ARCHITECTURAL
DRAWING
OPTIONS FOR DESIGN

ARCHITECTURAL DRAWING
OPTIONS FOR DESIGN

Paul Laseau

Design Press

ACKNOWLEDGMENTS

A book such as this is only possible as the result of the generosity of many architects, designers, and illustrators who readily shared their work with me. The conversations we had while assembling the illustrations confirm the lively interest professionals have in drawing and communication. I especially want to thank Kevin Forseth, Steve Oles, and Jim Stutzman, who made considerable contributions to this effort.

I am particularly grateful to Becky Amato for help with gathering illustrations; to Paul Lew for his work on creating illustrations; to Gina Webster of Design Press for her help in assembling the book; and to my editor, Nancy Green, who initiated this project and had the patience to see it through.

This book is dedicated to Kirby Lockard and others who have doggedly pursued the promotion of drawings as a means to design, and to my family.

First Edition, First Printing
Copyright © 1991 by Paul Laseau
Printed in the United States of America

Library of Congress Cataloging-in-Publication Data

Laseau, Paul, 1937-
    Architectural drawing : options for design / Paul Laseau.
      p. cm.
    Includes bibliographical references.
    ISBN 0-8306-7008-4
    ISBN 0-8306-8008-X (pbk.)
    1. Architectural drawing. 2. Architectural design. I. Title.
    NA2700.L33 1990   90-33795
    720′.28′4—dc20   CIP

Design Press offers posters and The Cropper, a device for cropping artwork, for sale. For information, contact Mail-order Department. Design Press books are available at special discounts for bulk purchases for sales promotions, fund raisers, or premiums. For details contact Special Sales Manager. Questions regarding the content of the book should be addressed to:

Design Press
11 West 19th Street
New York, NY 10011

Design Press books are published by Design Press, an imprint of TAB BOOKS.
TAB BOOKS is a Division of McGraw-Hill, Inc.
The Design Press logo is a trademark of TAB BOOKS.

Illustrations not otherwise credited are by the author.

CONTENTS

PREFACE

Throughout the history of architectural design, drawing has been a principal means of visualizing design solutions and guiding the process of bringing those solutions to constructed reality. Drawing is such an integral part of designing that we may often take it for granted. When the modern movement became commonly accepted as contemporary architectural practice during the decades after the Second World War, drawing standards, techniques, and applications became rather uniform. Acceptable use of drawing in support of design was familiar, predictable, and comfortable, Recently, a new awareness of drawings and a re-examination of their role and impact on design has resulted from two forces: the avant garde movements of the post-modern period and the extraordinary expansion of drawing means derived from the current revolution in computing and communication technologies. The resulting proliferation of drawing tools and the emerging visual literacy of clients and the public compels architects and designers to expand their concepts of design communication and re-examine their drawing options.

In this book I have attempted to provide a comprehensive view of the roles of drawing in architectural design; my concern is more with the meanings drawings have for design and thinking, than with drawing tools or techniques, which are addressed by many excellent existing books. The power of drawing options lies more in the perceptions gained by the designer than in the physical characteristics of the technology. After proposing expectations that architects and designers should consider for drawings, the book provides an overview of traditional conventions and then discusses several means of expanding drawing options: view, subject, setting, medium, and abstraction. The closing chapter reviews currently evolving explorations of drawing options.

While collecting the illustrations for this book, I was struck by the variety and vitality of drawings used by architects and designers. The search for new directions in design appears to be accompanied by an equally exciting search for new means of seeing and communicating. Equally impressive were the generosity and enthusiasm with which these professionals shared their drawings with me. I am most grateful for their help. With the pace at which drawing technologies are evolving and the degree of current experimentation, it is difficult to cover all drawing options in one book. However, I hope you will share my delight in evolving drawing options and undertake your own explorations of the potentials of drawing.

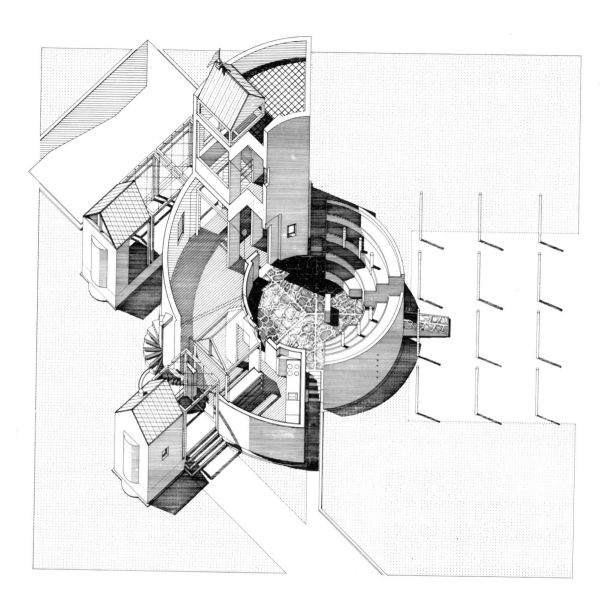

1 – 1   Axonometric
drawing by Brian Healy.
Healy House. Brian Healy,
Architects.

THE ROLES OF DRAWING IN DESIGN   ▌

Most architects recognize the importance of a design vocabulary, namely physical media of built environment or a set of choices for formal responses to meet human needs. Much of their formal training and professional lives are devoted to understanding and broadening their design vocabulary. Study of design and designers also reveals the strong influence of drawings as integral parts of a design process. It is logical then that designers would seek a parallel expansion of their drawing vocabulary in order to have the broadest set of tools to support design thinking.

The purpose of this book is to present the designer with a broad set of choices available in drawing. The review of drawing options is intended to give architects and designers ready access to a number of drawing possibilities that directly enhance design thinking. This is not so much a "how-to-do-it" book as it is a "what-is-possible" book. It is an introduction to the potential of drawings in their widest array, an orientation that will encourage the architect/designer to examine and experiment with the utility of drawings. The book serves as a reference to the many resources, including books on available techniques, conventions, and media.

This work also addresses the qualitative aspects of drawings and their multiple levels of communication and meaning. Rather than dwelling on technical description, emphasis is placed on the importance of the relationship between drawings and the thinking process of the designer. Drawings of themselves, as lines on paper or in electronic media, have no meaning except that which we give them. Drawings cannot affect us or be effective unless we attach meanings to them. To the extent that we understand the meanings that drawings can have within our processes of thinking, we enlarge their importance and contribution to design while enriching the design experience.

1–2 Freehand sketch by Bon Hui Uy. Ink. Lahaini Maui, HI.

1–3 Design sketch by Bon Hui Uy. Felt pen with pencil. Grasslands Housing, Mt. Pleasant, NY. Pokorny and Pertz, Architects.

The most commonly recognized role of drawings in design is as representation. We think of drawings as models for either an existing or anticipated reality; we see them as a miniaturization of the much larger reality of environment. In this view they also serve as a documentation of various stages in the design process, from schematic design to preliminary design, design development, contract documents, and shop drawings. It is important that we expand this concept of drawings and their role to include drawing as seeing, process, and thinking. Each of these skills affects the depth and breadth of design exploration and enriches the final results.

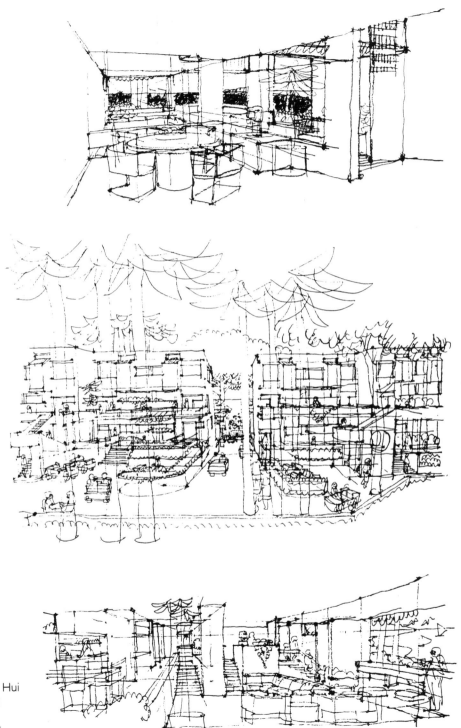

1 – 4 through 1 – 6
Design sketches by Bon Hui
Uy. Pencil. Dart, HI. Au
Smith & Haworth Ltd.,
Architects.

DRAWING AS SEEING

To be effective architectural designers, we must first understand environment, the medium in which we work. We must be able to perceive and make distinctions about the vocabulary and grammar of the existing environment. Just as the composer must convert experiences into musical notation as a step toward mature compositions, the architect must convert environmental experience into the graphic notations that are the media of architectural design.

Drawing as seeing goes beyond description to analysis, understanding, and critical judgment. Designing is essentially composed of two parts, generation and evaluation; the designer must both form proposals and assess their suitability. Edmund Burke Feldman has identified *understanding* as the chief goal of artistic criticism (including architectural criticism): "We wish to find a way of looking at objects of art and thinking about them which will yield the maximum of knowledge about their real or alleged merits. Works of art yield information to the trained viewer, and this information is useful in the forming of critical judgments."* In pursuit of the understanding of architecture through drawing, we can consider the four key stages of the critical performance described by Feldman: description, formal analysis, interpretation, and judgment.

Description is an accounting or inventory of the features and characteristics of a design or environment. It is the process of simple, direct observation of concrete, indisputable realities, such as size, shape, color, and position. In graphic language description requires sketches of architecture that are comprehensive, reasonably accurate, true to scale and proportion, clear, and revealing.

Formal analysis describes the operation of principles embodied in the architectural design. We try to go beyond the basic description and point out the qualities of line, shape, color, rhythm, and illumination responsible for our experience of the architecture. The description of these qualities (including proportion, scale, sequence, and composition) is, of necessity, heavily reliant on drawings. The interactive nature and spatial distribution of these qualities requires the simultaneous representation found in graphic communication. The more abstract types of drawings are particularly useful for visual representation of formal analysis.

*Edmund Burke Feldman, *Art as Image and Idea* (Englewood Cliffs, NJ: Prentice-Hall, Inc., 1967), 444.

4

I – 7 Freehand sketch by
John J. Desmond. Ink.
Durham Cathedral.

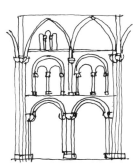

I – 8 Rhythm study.

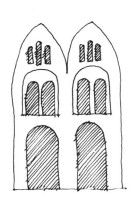

I – 9 Composition study.

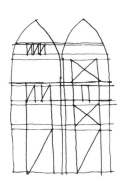

I – 10 Proportion study.

5

1 – 11 Design sketch by Bon Hui Uy. Pencil. Town House Project, Queensland, Australia. Media Five Ltd., Architect.

1 – 12 Exterior perspective by William Kirby Lockard. From *Design Drawing* by William Kirby Lockard.

Interpretation involves the discovery of the meanings embodied in a design and the formation of assumptions about the relevance of those meanings to our lives and the overall human condition. Drawings can be an important means of conveying interpretations of an environment, such as its identity, character, or mood.

Judgment involves ranking a work of architecture with respect to other works in its category and deciding its relative merit with regard to the basic criteria of utility, economy, and aesthetics. Because the basic operational condition for judgment is comparison, drawing options must be carefully selected and applied to support judgment. The consistent use of a graphic language or drawing style can markedly facilitate critical evaluation.

1 – 13 Circulation diagram.

1 – 14 through 1 – 16
Interior perspective studies
by William Kirby Lockard.
From *Design Drawing* by
William Kirby Lockard.

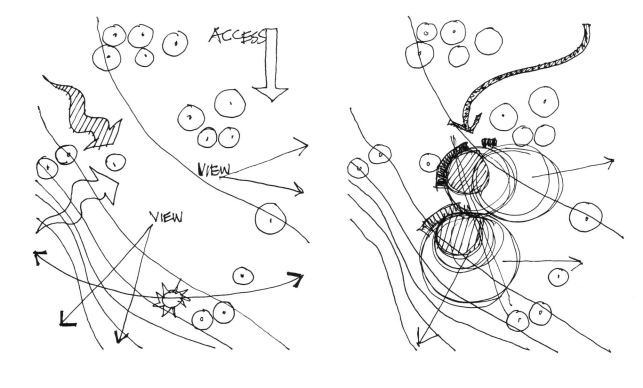

DRAWING AS PROCESS

Fundamental to all human endeavors is their reliance on human communication. As one form of human activity, design processes incorporate a wide spectrum of human communications from information to innuendo. From the particular focus of architectural design on spatial arrangement and complex interactive systems there have evolved highly elaborate, visually based forms of communication, normally supported by drawings.

As a means of problem solving, drawings support problem analysis and definition, generation of alternative responses, design evaluation, design development, and design implementation. As a management aid, drawings provide a framework or common referent for integrating the contributions of a diverse group of participants in the design process, ranging from the client to the contractor. As aesthetic artifacts in their own right, drawings can also reinforce shared values and motivations.

1 – 17 Problem analysis sketch.

1 – 18 Problem definition sketch.

1 – 19 Design response sketch.

1 – 20 Design evaluation sketch.

1 – 21. Design development sketch.

1 – 22. Design implementation sketch.

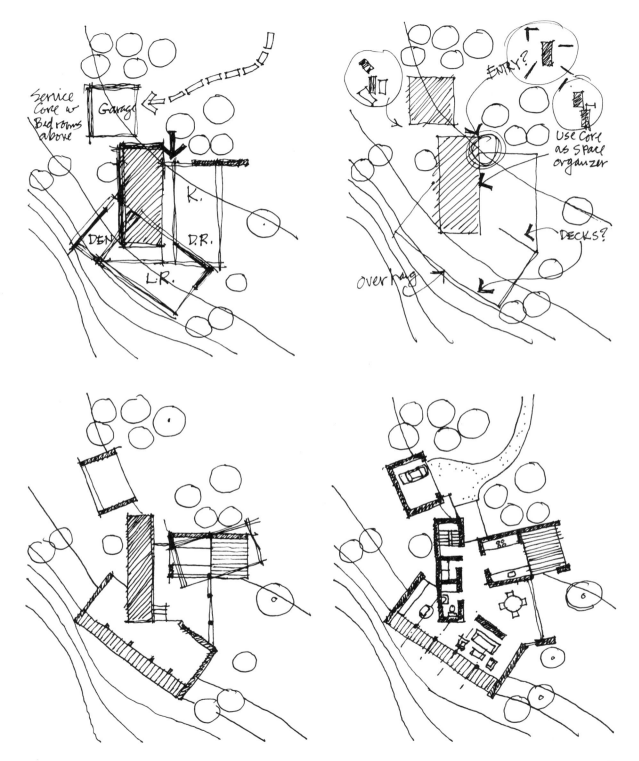

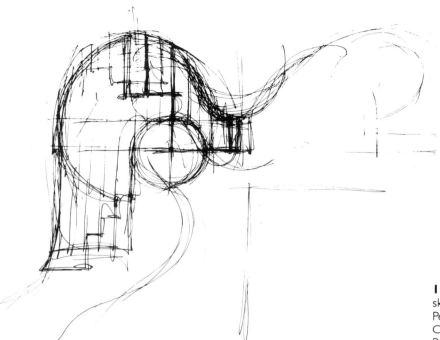

DRAWING AS THINKING

Traditional scientific philosophy has, to an extent, conditioned us to describe phenomena in terms of separate categories or parts and the distinguishing characteristics or identities of the parts. Thus, it has been our habit to dwell on the distinctions between thinking and vision rather than their interaction. Modern research in cognitive psychology and brain physiology has, however, established a view of an integrated system of visual thinking, a form of thinking that uses the products of vision—seeing, imagining, and drawing. When thinking becomes externalized in the form of a drawn image, it can be said to have become graphic.

The process of graphic thinking can be seen as a conversation with ourselves involving the sketched image on paper, the eye, the brain, and the hand. The potential of graphic thinking lies in the continuous cycling of information from drawing to eye to brain to hand and back to drawing.

If the impact of media on meaning or content is recognized, the role of drawing as thinking is potentially the most far-reaching and profound instrument for change in the evolution of future design processes. Studies of creativity and invention highlight visualization and shifts in perception as vital catalysts. Drawings can be used both to provoke specific thoughts and to alter thinking patterns purposely to promote imagination and innovation.

I – 24 Design sketches by Peter Eisenman. Pen. House III, from *House of Cards* by Peter Eisenman.

I – 25 Design study sketches by Gunnar Birkerts. Ferguson Residence. Gunnar Birkerts, Architect.

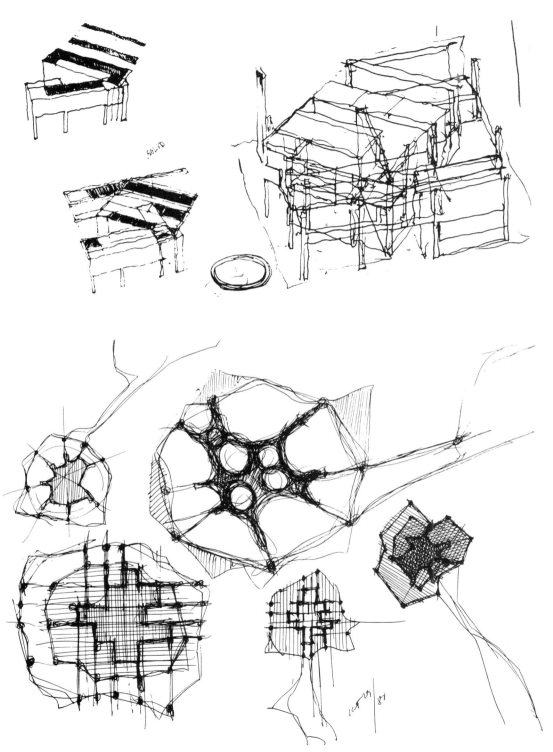

11

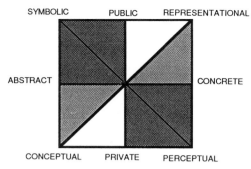

SYMBOLIC　　PUBLIC　　REPRESENTATIONAL

ABSTRACT　　　　　　　CONCRETE

CONCEPTUAL　　PRIVATE　　PERCEPTUAL

1 – 26 Scope of design communication, based on a diagram by Paul Stevenson Oles.

THE DIMENSIONS OF DESIGN DRAWING

Steve Oles, architect and noted architectural illustrator, has developed a diagram to show the dimensions of design drawing. It provides a good base for an overview of the possibilities for applying drawings to design processes. The options range from perceptual to conceptual, abstract to concrete, symbolic to representational, and private to public. The darker gray indicates areas of extensive development of conventions, whereas white indicates areas of little development thus far.

Perception to Conception

Perceptual drawings help us to anticipate the experience of something being designed. For example, perspectives tell us the scale, shape, lighting, detail, textures, and patterns that one would experience within a space. Perceptual drawings are valuable not only as ways to describe and imitate the reality of an experience that might be gained from a work, but also as an important way to examine and understand existing environments. Perceptual drawings connect the designer and the design process to the reality of the world we seek to improve. That is why accuracy and faithfulness in representing the objects or environments as they will be is extremely important, certainly more important than the mere attractiveness of the sketch or drawing itself.

For the beginning student, in the short run, it is sometimes beneficial to develop an ability to produce a pleasing sketch, one in which the student can take pride. But failure to develop from that level, failure to search for an accurate definition of design form, can be crippling to the process of design. If, in the search for superficial attractiveness, we jeopardize or interfere with the credibility of the drawing, we cheat ourselves as designers. The doctoring of representational drawings to sell a project to a client is bad enough, but to fool ourselves in the use of drawings hampers our development of critical judgment. To use drawing as an effective surrogate for the anticipated realities of an architectural design, we must construct a reliable relationship between drawing and reality.

1 – 27 Design sketch draft by William Kirby Lockard. Marker on tracing paper. From *Design Drawing Experiences* by William Kirby Lockard.

1 – 28 Rendered design perspective by William Kirby Lockard. Ink. From *Design Drawing Experiences* by William Kirby Lockard.

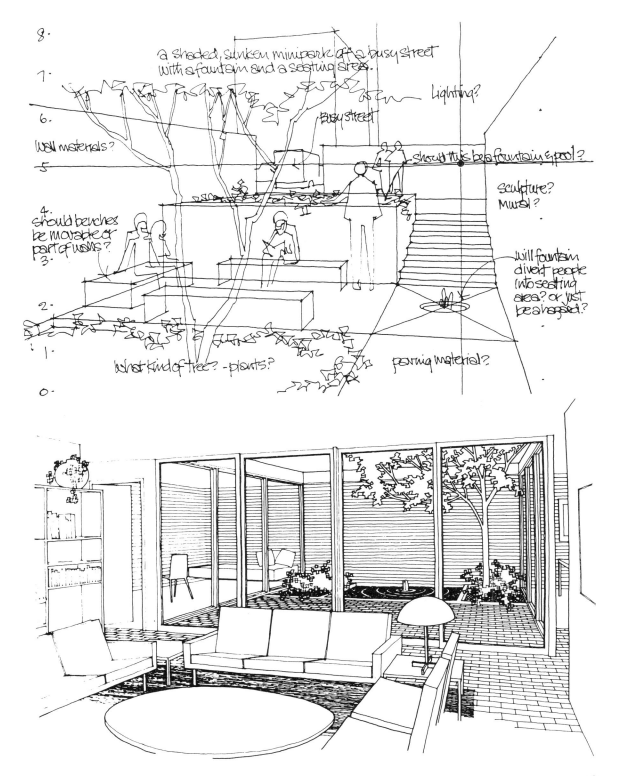

8.

7.

a shaded, sunken minipark off a busy street
with a fountain and a seating area.

Lighting?

6.

Busy street

Wall materials?

5.

should this be a fountain & pool?

sculpture?
Mural?

4. should benches
be movable or
part of walls?

3.

Will fountain
divert people
into seating
area? or just
be a hazard?

2.

1.

What kind of tree? -plants?

paving material?

0.

13

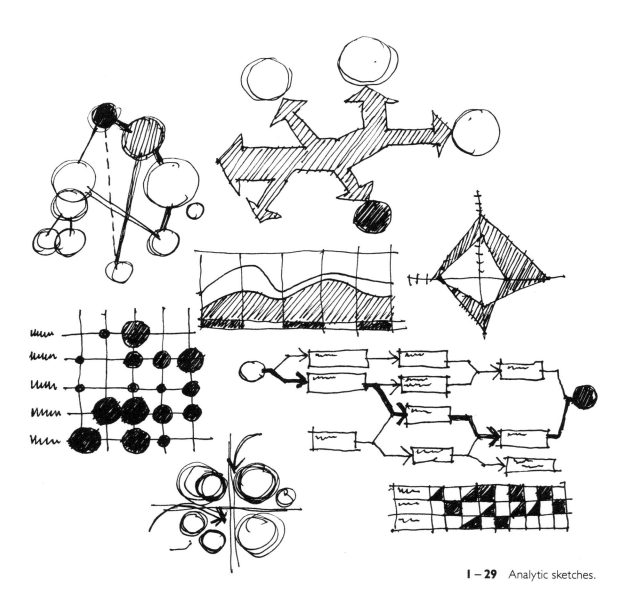

1–29 Analytic sketches.

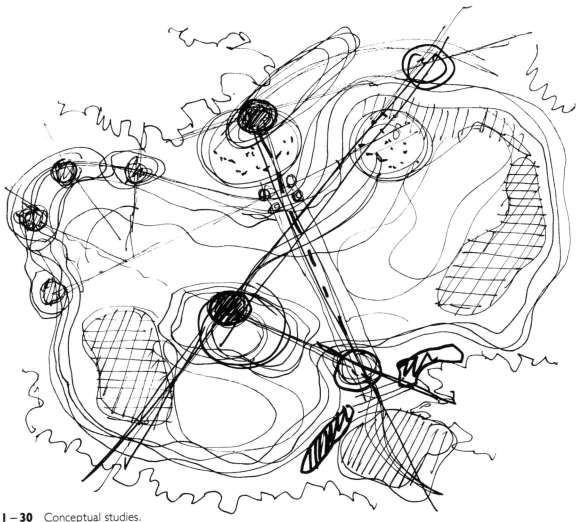

I – 30 Conceptual studies.

Conceptual Drawings

If perceptual drawings allow us to experience what has been designed, conceptual drawings provide a window on how we undertake designing and how we think about design. Conceptual drawings are used to record such things as the nature of the design problem, the context in which we design, the pattern of needs, design objectives, patterns of use, design concepts, geometric order, scale, rhythm, proportion, and a wide list of concerns that we must juggle in our minds during the design process. Because of the scope and complexity of ideas one must synthesize simultaneously while designing, conceptual communication is necessarily more abstract, symbolic, economical, and flexible.

15

Abstract to Concrete

This dimension of drawing reflects the range of focus of the designer, from the general to the specific. The use of more abstract drawings in the early stages of design leaves open options for the specific realization of general concepts. For example, if a drawing defines simply the volume and general proportion of a space, it sustains many possibilities, including the definition of the enclosure, orientation, lighting, and other attributes of the space. The more abstract the drawing, the more options remain open. At the other end of the scale, concrete drawings summarize the specific decisions about the design that allow testing of the design against a number of specific criteria, such as appearance, constructibility, and feasibility.

16

1 – 31 through 1 – 33
Facade studies.

1 – 34 Freehand sketch.
Felt pen on cartridge paper.
Office building, Shrewsbury,
England.

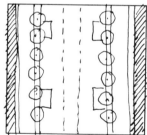

Symbolic to Representational

Some drawings are used to describe the physical world accurately rather than our perception or experience of it. Other drawings use symbols to stand in for physical objects or processes. The impact or effectiveness of these latter symbolic drawings is proportional to the richness of experiences or immediacy of realities that the designer can associate with the symbols. For the beginning student, symbolic drawings are of limited use; but the mature architect relies increasingly on the economy of drawings that provide the minimum amount of information necessary for design thinking to proceed.

1 – 35 Design sketch by Bon Hui Uy. Felt pen. Bellevue Environs Study, New York, NY. Davis Brody & Associates, Architects.

1 – 36 Plan diagram.

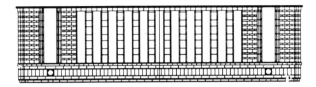

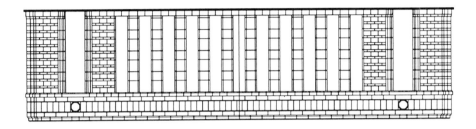

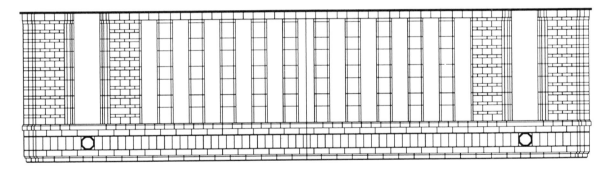

1–37 Facade studies by Jim Stutzman. Computer graphic. WPA/Terre Haute, IN. Stutzman and Associates, Architects.

Most experienced designers can confirm the importance of direct exposure to the construction of environments as we design them. Designing as you build provides direct exposure to the relationship between design ideas and their built consequences. In current architectural practice, such exposure is rare. One possible substitute for such experience is the study of buildings using full-scale representational drawings of their components. While this approach is used sparingly today, computer drawing, with its ease of multiple-scale printout, will make such drawings a practical option in the near future.

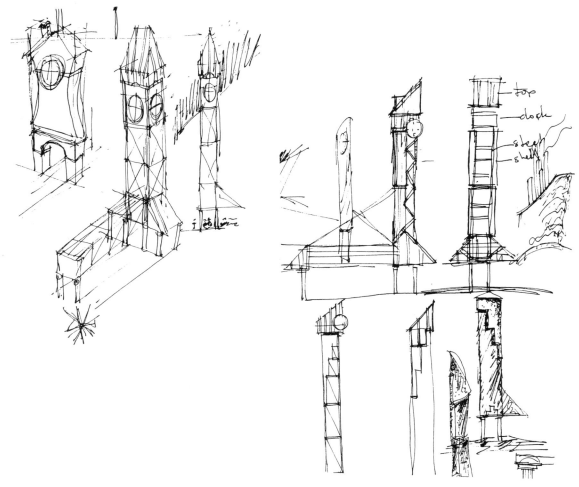

Private to Public

The appeal of the heroic image of the individual designer/architect might explain the traditional emphasis placed by teachers and writers on the use of drawings by the individual designer for his private design and thinking process. But in reality drawings can and usually do come into play in the design and thinking processes of groups of people, providing the public access to design as well. The range of drawing usage from the very private individual level to that of the very open public use in community meetings requires a similar range of drawing styles and types to meet the varying needs.

The form of more private drawings reflects the fast pace at which they are created in order to keep up with the thinking process. They are often open-ended and provocative, rather than conclusive, to stimulate the creative process.

1–38 and 1–39 Design sketches by Harry Eggink. Felt pen. Clock Tower Studies, Elkhart, IN.

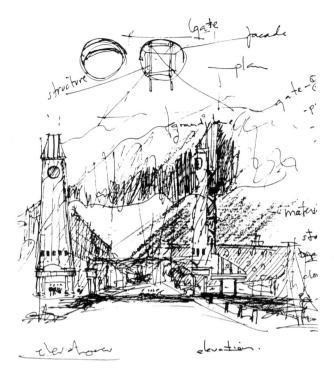

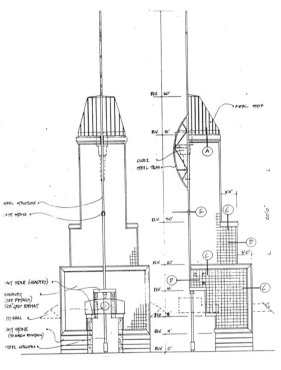

1–40 Design sketch by Harry Eggink. Felt pen. Clock Tower Studies, Elkhart, IN.

1–41 Elevations by Harry Eggink. Felt pen. Clock Tower Studies, Elkhart, IN. Harry Eggink, Architect.

Public drawings must accommodate a more deliberate review or scrutiny of design, recognizing the range of visual sophistication in an audience. Like all communication, public drawings must be designed and conceived, adjusted and tailored to the audience, keeping in mind the primary purpose of opening up communication channels rather than simply presenting the designer's side of a story. Public drawings share with private drawings the purpose of discovery. They are a means for the architect, designer, client, and users to develop a better understanding of both the design problem and the possible solutions.

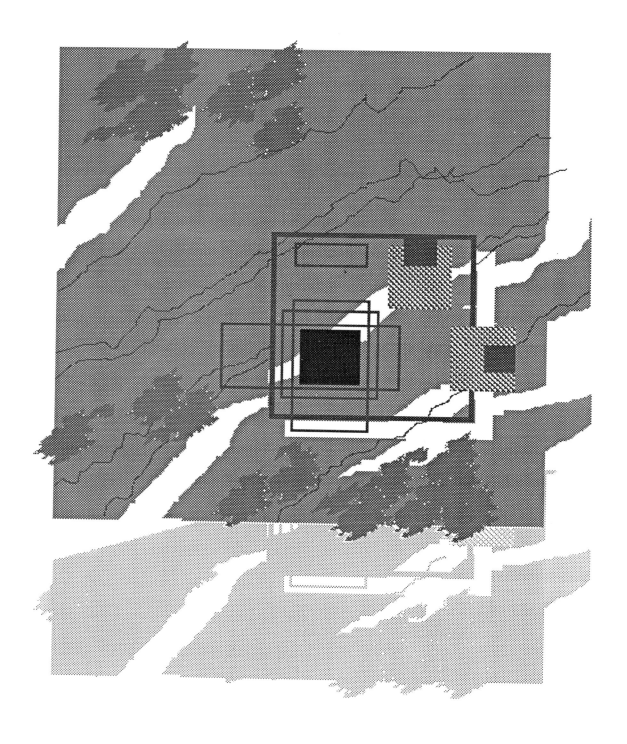

1–42 Design study.
Computer graphic.

THE FUTURE OF DRAWING

In recent years there has been overwhelming preoccupation with and alarm over the impact of computers and other technology on the role of drawing. The concerns range from the loss of the personal touch to the fear that human thinking will become subservient to machines. Computers and technology certainly offer new possibilities, but they share a basic characteristic with tools we have adopted throughout history: they are not self-defining. It is the meaning *we* find in new tools and the purposes *we* assign them that will determine their contribution and their role in design and drawing.

Electronic drawing media are developing very rapidly. Machines will become more sophisticated, and the differences we worry about now will not likely be of lasting concern. If we develop the necessary techniques, electronic drawing will be as sensitive as conventional drawings but possibly via quite different means. We do not expect the same results from a stick of charcoal as we do from a fountain pen; nevertheless, we expect creativity to be equally possible in both charcoal and ink. Certain kinds of drawing, seen narrowly as media, will become less important. But drawing, seen as a fundamental act of giving visibility and tangibility to ideas, can only grow and expand.

This book discusses drawings in two main dimensions. It moves from the more familiar conventions—sections, elevations, paraline projections, and perspectives—to the more complex and innovative types of drawings, which challenge our ways of seeing and thinking. From the simple structures of basic conventions, we will also explore other dimensions of drawing such as scale, focus, framing, definition, and abstraction.

Books about drawing have proliferated in the last two decades; why offer yet another book on drawing? Taken as a group, these books present a wide range of information about the creation and practical applications of conventional drawings; these books also have provided an informal consensus about the meaning and scope of design drawing, which could discourage further invention or the extension of the possibilities in drawing. This book attempts to take a fresh look at drawing in its various dimensions in order to awaken creativity, and reemphasize the important role of the individual's choices in the continuing evolution of drawing media.

The most critical function of drawings is that of externalizing our thinking in time and place, of giving form to ideas. The value of placing thoughts outside our heads is that we can then look at them from a different perspective. We are able to reflect on them, to absorb them, and to reconsider them. Just as different instruments render different experiences of a piece of music, different drawings have the potential to give us different understandings of our ideas.

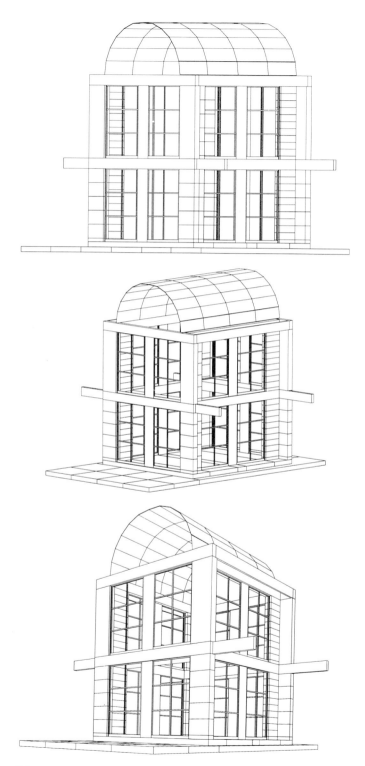

2 – 1 Orthographic, paraline, and perspective projections by Kevin Forseth. Computer graphic (Architrion). House I.

DRAWING CONVENTIONS

2

Conventions play a central role in the realm of drawings, as a context for understanding, as the "glue" in most drawings. They represent a common language that allows us to understand someone else's drawings, or at least to begin to organize in our mind what is being communicated. They provide a base order from which we can branch out and discover new ways of looking at things. Drawing conventions have evolved from historically practical needs within the design process, such as the ability to establish scale, proportion, dimension; the need to identify parts, or portray the views one might see when moving through an environment; and the need to evaluate a building design qualitatively and quantitatively. The terms *elevation, section, plan,* and *perspective* each have a commonly understood meaning and represent a shared expectation among designers.

There are three basic types of conventions: orthographic projection, paraline projection, and perspective projection. Orthographic projections document space by presenting a series of two-dimensional views that, taken as a group, give an accurate, to-scale representation of the total building. Paraline projections begin to capture the three-dimensionality of space while retaining a consistent, uniform scale. Perspective projections deal more with the actual experience of three-dimensionality; they do not concern themselves with a constant scale but rather reveal relative scale as seen in space. The role of drawing conventions could be compared to that of the conventions for courses in a meal, in that they provide a broad framework and basic categorization within which one can explore and invent numerous variations in type or media.

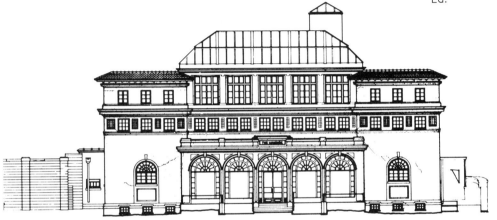

2 – 2 Facade by Jack E. Boucher, 1983. Photo. Maurice Bath House, Hot Springs National Park, AK. From *Recording Historic Structures*, John A. Burns, Ed.

2 – 3 Elevation by Gregory C. McCall, 1985. Ink. Maurice Bath House, Hot Springs National Park, AK. From *Recording Historic Structures*, John A. Burns, Ed.

ORTHOGRAPHIC PROJECTIONS

Orthographic projections are similar to photographs in that they project visible environments onto a two-dimensional surface. They differ from photographs in that elements shown on the drawing surface retain their relative existing scale so that even those objects or spaces that are farther away, appearing smaller to the camera, retain their actual size when projected forward. A door that is seven feet high is always drawn to be seven feet high, no matter how far away it is from our viewpoint.

The term *orthographic* refers to being perpendicular or having right angles, a recognition that traditional orthographic views are taken at a ninety-degree angle to the surface being viewed. Orthographic projections are created by constructing an imaginary transparent plane between the viewer and the subject and then projecting all items at their relative scales forward to the back of a transparent plane. The orthographic convention has two basic variations: the elevation, in which the transparent plane is between the

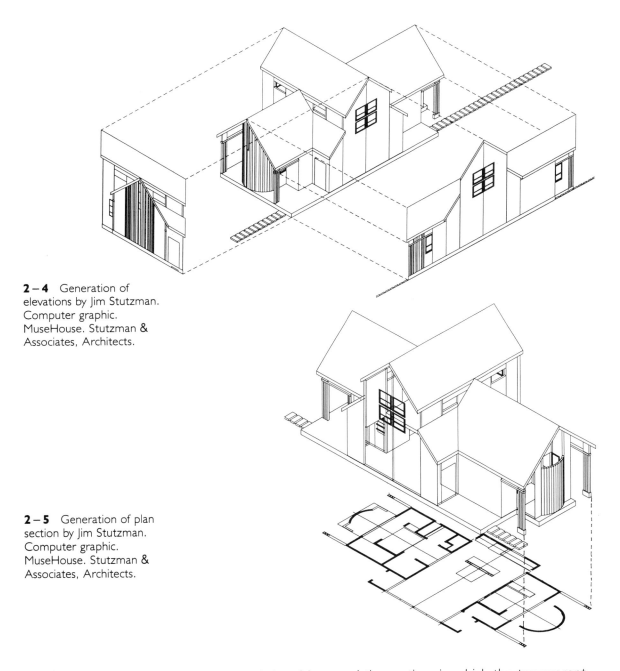

2 − 4 Generation of elevations by Jim Stutzman. Computer graphic. MuseHouse. Stutzman & Associates, Architects.

2 − 5 Generation of plan section by Jim Stutzman. Computer graphic. MuseHouse. Stutzman & Associates, Architects.

viewer and the object; and the section, in which the transparent plane cuts through the object. Other familiar views are derived from either elevations or sections. The roof plan is actually a horizontal elevation, looking down on the top of a building or space, and the plan view is actually a horizontal section.

Elevation

Of all the drawing options available, one of the oldest, the elevation, is still the most clear, direct, and simple means of communicating a realistic view of architecture to the widest audience. Realism is achieved by careful attention to recognizable attributes of the subject of the drawing: scale, composition, proportion, repetition, rhythm, texture, color, shape, pattern, detail.

2–6 Rendering by John J. Desmond. Ink on mylar. Louisiana State University, Center for Engineering. John J. Desmond & Associates, Architects.

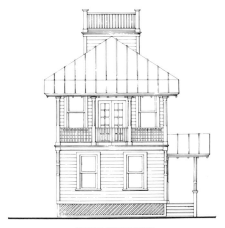

FRONT ELEVATION

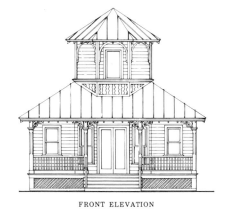

FRONT ELEVATION

SIDE ELEVATION

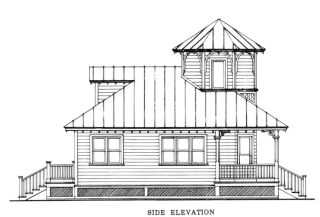

SIDE ELEVATION

2 – 7 Elevations by Orr &
Taylor. Ink. Rosewalk
Cottages. Orr & Taylor,
Architects.

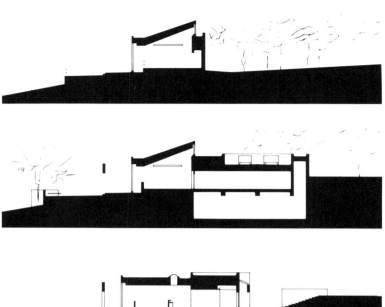

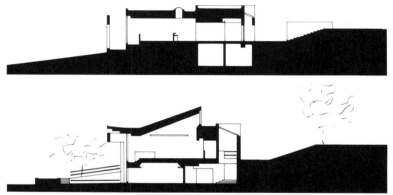

2 – 8 Building-site sections by Mitchell/Giurgola. Ink. Tredyffrin Public Library. Mitchell/Giurgola, Architects.

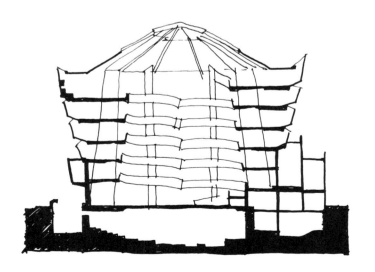

2 – 9 Sketch section. Felt pen. Solomon R. Guggenheim Museum, New York, NY. Frank Lloyd Wright, Architect.

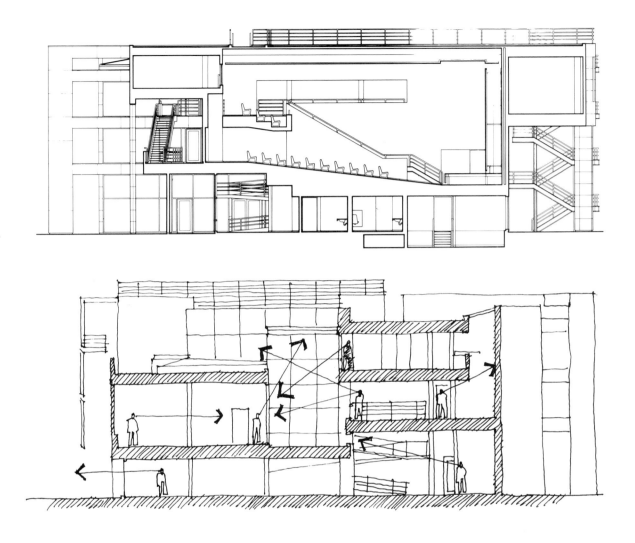

Vertical Section

Probably the most underrated drawing type, the section provides a rapid means to depict scale, enclosure, light, spatial character, and spatial experience. While sections lack the degree of definition of three-dimensional space provided by a perspective or paraline projection, they are more effective than a plan section in examining the relationships between people and space. Showing human figures in space helps the viewer imagine being in the space. The simulation of the experience of the space can be further enhanced by indicating possible lines of view for potential inhabitants.

2 – 10 Section by Richard Meier & Partners. Ink. The Atheneum, New Harmony, IN. Richard Meier & Partners, Architects.

2 – 11 Section sketch. Felt pen. The Atheneum, New Harmony, IN. Richard Meier & Partners, Architects.

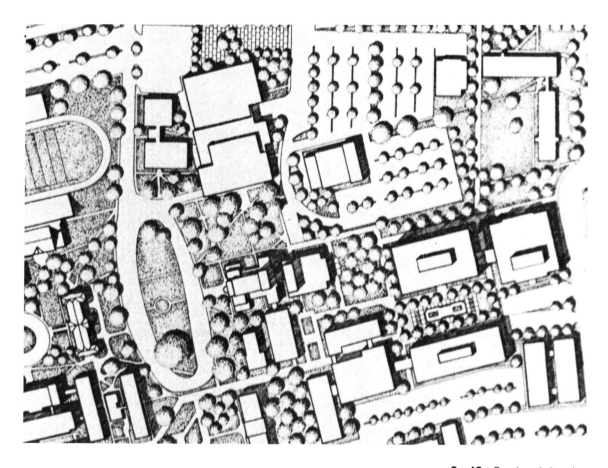

2 – 12 Rendered site plan by John J. Desmond. Ink. Southeastern Louisiana University Campus Study. John J. Desmond & Associates, Architects.

Plan Elevation

These views, taken along a vertical rather than a horizontal axis, are usually referred to as roof plans or site plans. They provide an easily understood overview of a subject and basic orientation for the viewer. Plan elevations can also illustrate the physical context of the subject. In later chapters we will see how this convention can provide the base for a variety of conceptual drawings or diagrams.

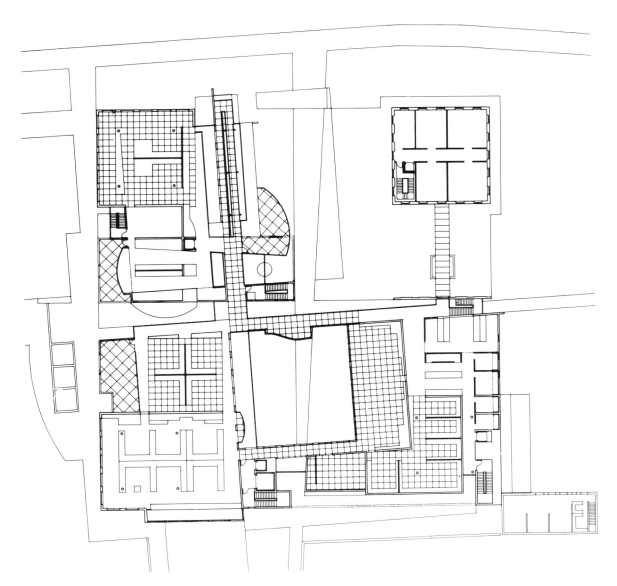

2 – 13 Upper-level plan by
Richard Meier & Partners.
Ink. Park Gate, Museum for
the Decorative Arts,
Frankfurt. Richard Meier &
Partners, Architects.

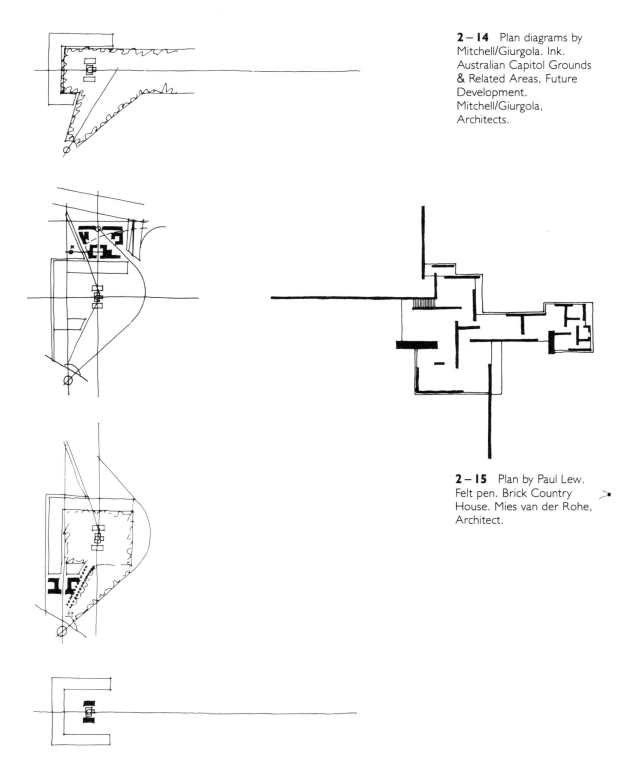

2 – 14 Plan diagrams by Mitchell/Giurgola. Ink. Australian Capitol Grounds & Related Areas, Future Development. Mitchell/Giurgola, Architects.

2 – 15 Plan by Paul Lew. Felt pen. Brick Country House. Mies van der Rohe, Architect.

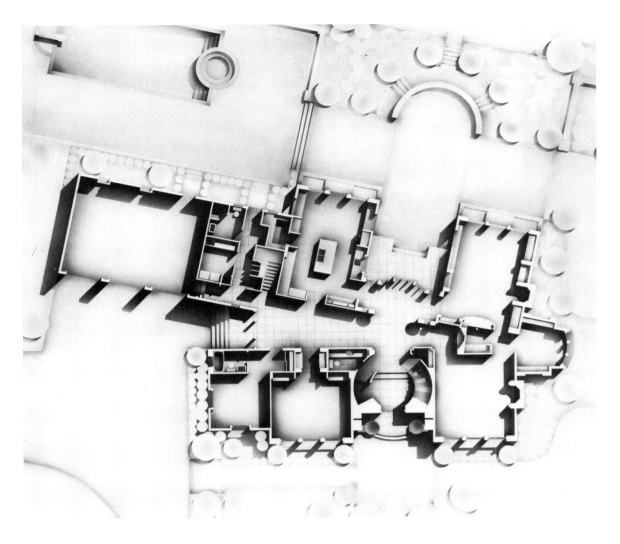

Plan Section

Traditionally referred to simply as the plan, this view is generated, like the vertical section, by making a cut through the subject. As the most familiar of drawing conventions, it is probably the most misused or least effectively used. Many designers and, in particular, design students are content to use the plan as a diagraming tool to address organizational rather than experiential concerns of architecture. Properly rendered, plans can provide a heightened sense of the qualities of spaces while retaining a comprehensive view and strong sense of orientation. While illustrated plans may include extensive detail, depiction of basic space and enclosure can also be achieved economically.

2 – 16 Rendered plan by Mark English. Air brush and pencil on canvas. Kahn Residence. House + House, Architects, San Francisco.

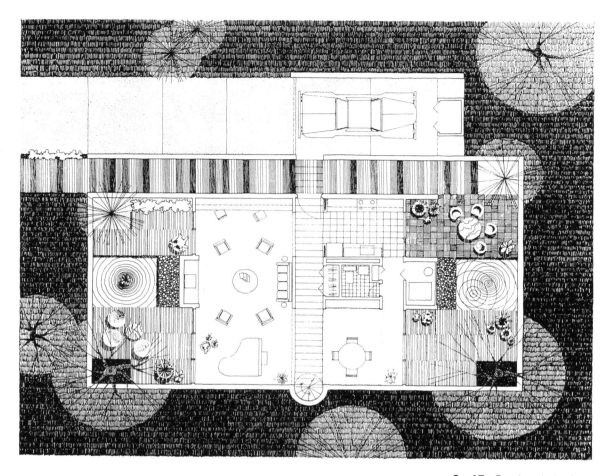

2−17 Rendered plan by Edward T. White. Ink. From *A Graphic Vocabulary for Architectural Presentation* by Edward T. White.

Scale

The most obvious attribute of orthographic projections, namely constant scale, is in fact its most powerful effect. Constant scale helps us to understand the relationships among all the parts of a building and their relationship to human scale. To take full advantage of orthographic projections as designers, we should be sensitive to the issue of scale and insert on the drawing various things that can allow us to appreciate the human scale of building, including human figures, furniture, and building parts that relate to human scale.

2−18 Section perspective by Croxton Collaborative. Ink on mylar. Headquarters Natural Resources Defense Council. Croxton Collaborative.

2−19 Illustrated section by William Kirby Lockard. Ink. From *Design Drawing* by William Kirby Lockard.

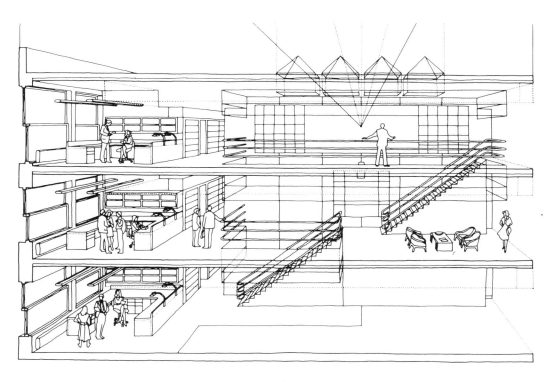

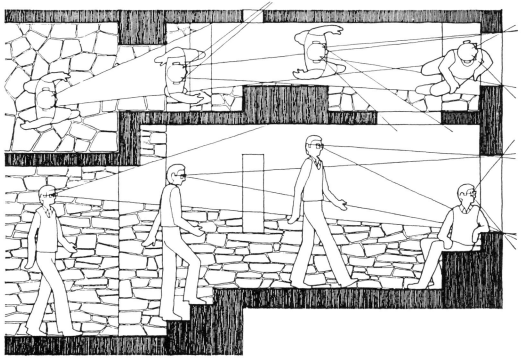

37

2 – 20 Plan with cast shadows by Lawrence Doane. Ink. Silicon Valley Financial Center Master Plan, San Jose, CA. Skidmore, Owings, and Merrill-San Francisco, Architects.

Depth

Orthographic projections often are rendered in a way that conveys the existence of the third dimension. Heavy outlining of major breaks in surfaces or the use of shadow-casting conventions are common ways of representing depth. An atmospheric sense of depth is created by varying the intensity of the rendering.

On occasion designers wish to eliminate any sense of depth in elevations. They sacrifice representation of three-dimensional space in order to focus on other issues, such as aesthetic unity. In these cases the various depth clues are carefully removed, and emphasis is placed on a consistent use of media throughout the drawing.

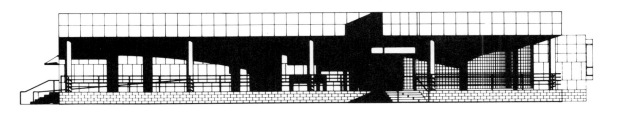

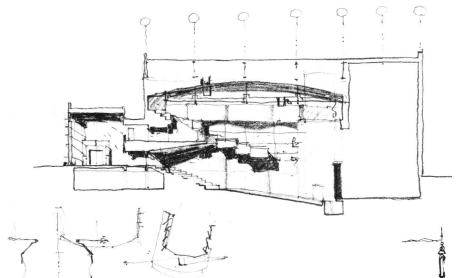

2 – 21 Elevation with shadows by Anthony Ames. Ink. Branch Library, Alpharetta, GA. Anthony Ames, Architect.

2 – 22 Rendered sketch section by Neil Denari. York College Theatre, Jamaica, Queens, NY. James Stewart Polshek and Partners, Architects.

2 – 23 Elevation sketch by Charles W. Moore. Ink. From *Body, Memory, and Architecture* by Kent C. Bloomer and Charles W. Moore.

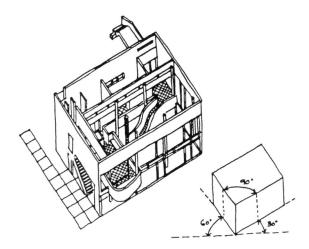

2 – 24 Plan projection. Felt pen. Shamberg House. Richard Meier & Partners, Architects.

PARALINE PROJECTIONS

Paraline projections create a sensation of three-dimensional space by projecting parallel lines from an orthographic projection. These drawings are arguably the easiest for an average person to understand because of their constant scale and angle of view and the provision of a comprehensive, rather than selective, view of the subject. They have the added virtue of being relatively easy to create.

Paraline drawings have enjoyed increasing popularity for presentations, particularly with designers who are more concerned with the conceptual or aesthetic unity of their projects than with the perceptual experience of spaces and forms. Their constant scale makes paraline drawings especially useful in taking advantage of the rapid duplication capabilities of computer graphics.

Plan Projection

The most commonly used form of paraline drawing, the plan projection does not represent the experience of being in a space; it provides a view from above the space similar to an aerial perspective. As one might expect, plan projections are constructed by projecting vertical elements up from a plan. The carefully drawn plan projection with the roof removed, as shown above, provides a sense of the three-dimensional quality of spaces while giving a detail view of the construction, enclosure, and other elements such as stairs, flooring, furniture, and fixtures. The view into the spaces can be adjusted by changing the angle of the generating plan.

2 – 25 Plan projection diagrams. Felt pen. Shamberg House. Richard Meier & Partners, Architects.

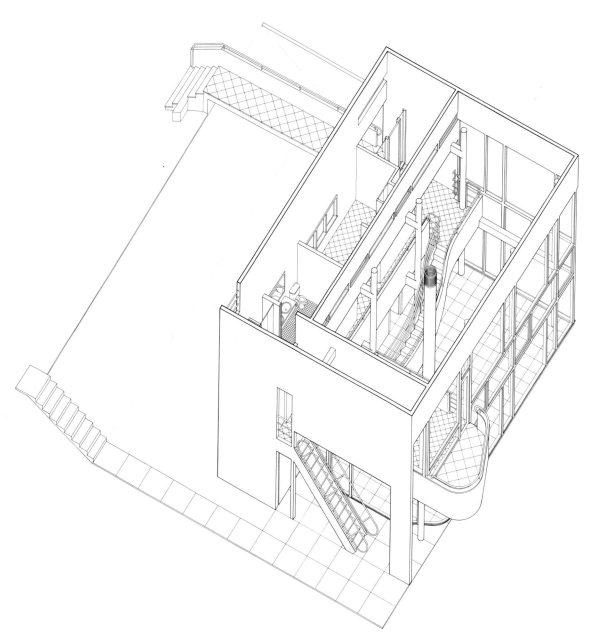

2 – 26 Plan projection by Richard Meier. Ink. Shamberg House. Richard Meier & Partners, Architects.

    This convention also provides a simple, effective means of illustrating analyses of architectural form. Even with a high degree of abstraction, these drawings retain a strong sense of the third dimension. Such diagrams clearly illustrate the organizing elements of a building, such as structure, enclosure, circulation, and functional zoning.

2 – 27 Elevation projection, based on Persian painting by Kamaluddin Bihzad, by Paul Lew. Felt pen.

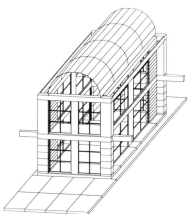

Elevation Projection

This convention was often used in traditional Oriental painting. In contrast to Western perspective, it gives the viewer equally detailed information about all parts of the scene. Rather than fixing the viewer in one position, this drawing allows a choice of many observation points. This impact of the drawing on the viewer's perceptions is an important consideration that will be discussed further as we consider more complex or nonconventional uses of drawings.

2 – 28 Elevation projection by Kevin Forseth. Computer graphic (Architrion). House I.

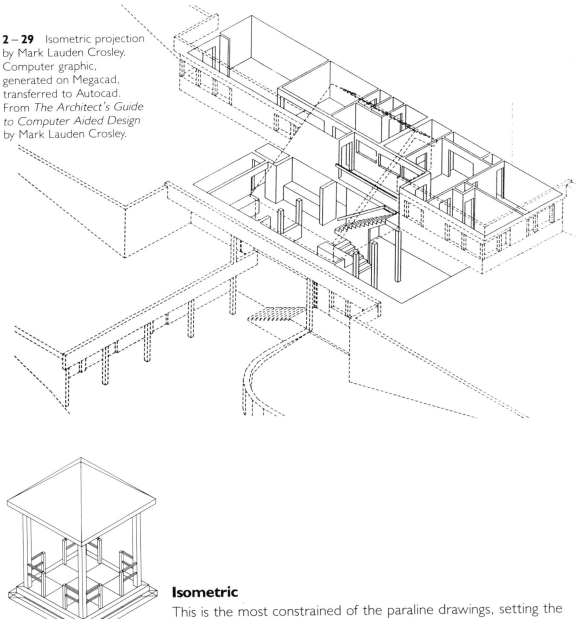

2 – 29 Isometric projection by Mark Lauden Crosley. Computer graphic, generated on Megacad, transferred to Autocad. From *The Architect's Guide to Computer Aided Design* by Mark Lauden Crosley.

2 – 30 Isometric projection by Paul Lew. Computer graphic. Gazebo.

Isometric

This is the most constrained of the paraline drawings, setting the three dimensions of space at equal angles to each other. Some designers prefer this convention because its appearance is similar to that of perspective, but it retains the ease of paraline construction. In freehand sketching, however, this similarity to perspective can lead to an annoying tendency to slip unwittingly back and forth between isometric and perspective conventions.

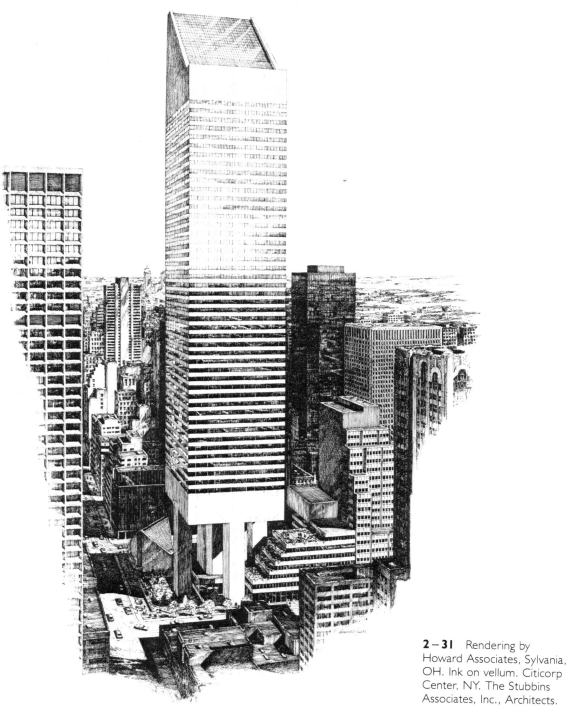

2–31 Rendering by Howard Associates, Sylvania, OH. Ink on vellum. Citicorp Center, NY. The Stubbins Associates, Inc., Architects.

2 – 32 and 2 – 33 Design sketch perspectives by William Kirby Lockard. Felt pen. From *Design Drawing Experiences* by William Kirby Lockard.

PERSPECTIVE PROJECTIONS

It is an interesting paradox that the perspective, the most written about type of drawing, is traditionally the most underutilized in the design process. An overview of the numerous books on perspective provides some insights. These books, for the most part, concentrate on techniques of constructing perspectives, promoting an interesting, elaborate ritual for the designer, illustrator, or draftsperson. Rarely is the purpose or the utility of perspectives discussed. Perspectives are also commonly associated with elaborate renderings for the benefit of clients and their promotional needs. These are generally representations of the building design after the design process is completed and the final idea is fixed.

Perhaps another contributing factor is that many architects see themselves as dealing primarily with the composition of space and forms, not with the experience of those spaces. Elevation and parallel projection drawings are favored over perspectives, which provide a viewpoint one would have standing in the environment. In spite of the promotion of perspective as a working tool for design by several authors, starting with Kirby Lockard and Phillip Thiel late in the 1960s, perspective continues to be underutilized in the process of design. Some researchers of environment and behavior feel that the avoidance of perspective is an indication that architects are more concerned with the stylistic issues relevant to their peers than the needs of clients, particularly their experience and use of the constructed architectural space.

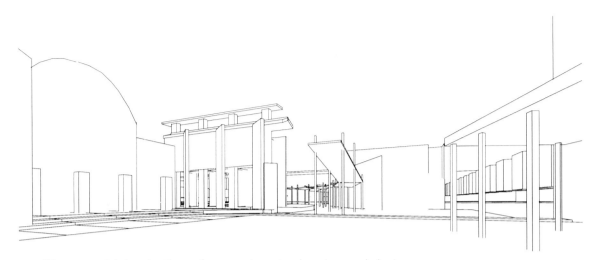

The recent introduction of computers to drawing and design may bring about the first large-scale adoption of perspective as a design tool. With the availability of perspective construction and three-dimensional graphic programs on microcomputers, one of the biggest obstacles to the use of perspectives, the time required to construct them, will be eliminated. Using three-dimensional computer graphics programs, one can construct a model of the environment with the computer. Several perspective views at different positions and directions can then be quickly produced, eliminating the time-consuming construction of separate conventional perspective drawings. This will encourage the creation of view sequences, representing the experience of moving through a building. Just as precision drafting in the beginning of this century brought a familiarity with plan and elevation views that encouraged people to sketch using similar conventions, the introduction of precision perspective generation on computers will encourage the use of sketch design studies. As architects become more familiar and comfortable with the perspective convention, they will be able to visualize designs in perspective. This is bound to benefit the design because it adds a significant dimension to the evaluation process, the simulation of the experience of the environment being designed. In the near future, we may see the common usage of shadow-casting and reflection-casting programs as additions to three-dimensional computer graphics, adding to the realism of the experience represented by perspective drawings. As these new perspective-generating tools become available, it will be important for designers to understand the different drawing tools and, more important, the purposes to which they might be applied in the process of design. The following discussion about various perspective conventions focuses on their utility in the realm of design.

2 – 34 through 2 – 36
Perspectives by Brendon Pollard. Computer graphic. Ball State University Student Commons Project, Muncie, IN.

47

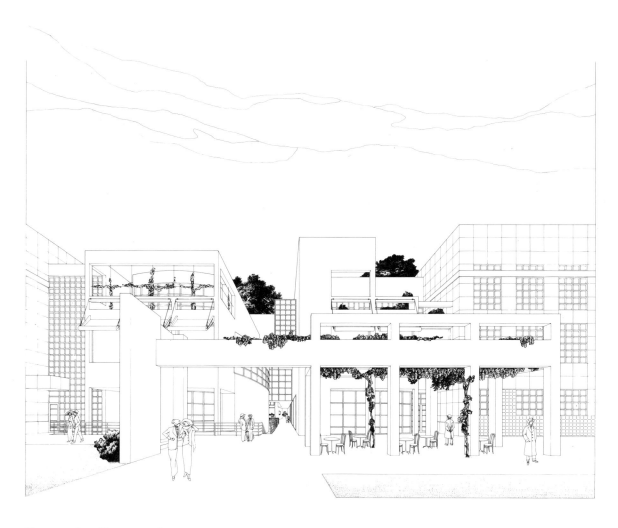

One-point Perspective

Probably the most easily adopted perspective drawing convention is the one-point perspective because of its proximity to orthographic projection. As in elevation drawings, the one-point perspective angle of view is at ninety degrees to the surface being viewed. Unlike the elevation, one-point perspective shows equal-sized objects as smaller in their viewed scale when they are more distant from the viewer. Much like the camera, perspective shows parallel lines as converging in the distance. The first of the perspective conventions invented during the Renaissance, one-point perspective creates a highly realistic view as one would see it from a single, fixed view-point. Although objects are shown in many scales as they appear at different distances from the viewer, all objects within the same plane retain their actual scale relationship to each other. This makes one-point perspective the easiest perspective convention to construct.

2 – 37 Perspective View by Richard Meier & Partners. Outdoor Cafe, Museum for the Decorative Arts, Frankfurt. Richard Meier & Partners, Architects.

2–38 Perspective by Steven Holl. Ink. Oceanfront House. Steven Holl, Architects.

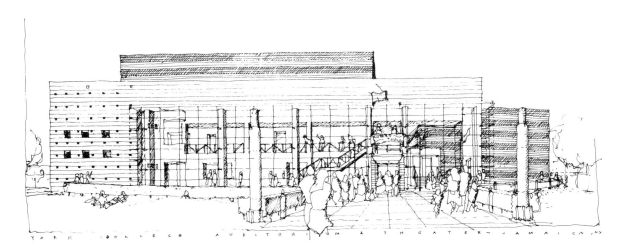

2–39 Perspective sketch by Neil Denari. Ink. York College Theatre. James Stewart Polshek and Partners, Architects.

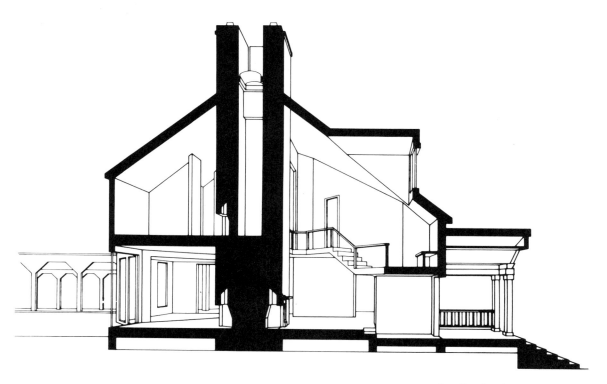

2 − 40 Section perspective by Gerald Allen. Ink. Smyth House, from *The Place of Houses* by Charles Moore, Gerald Allen and Donlyn Lyndon.

A convenient method for initiating a one-point perspective is to start with either an elevation or section drawing and project the environment in front of or behind the plane in which the elevation or section cut was made. Using the orthographic projection scale, one can establish the size of other objects in front of and behind that plane with a relatively accurate sense of scale. Orthographic projections provide a ready reference for the size and configuration of many of the objects being portrayed in the perspective.

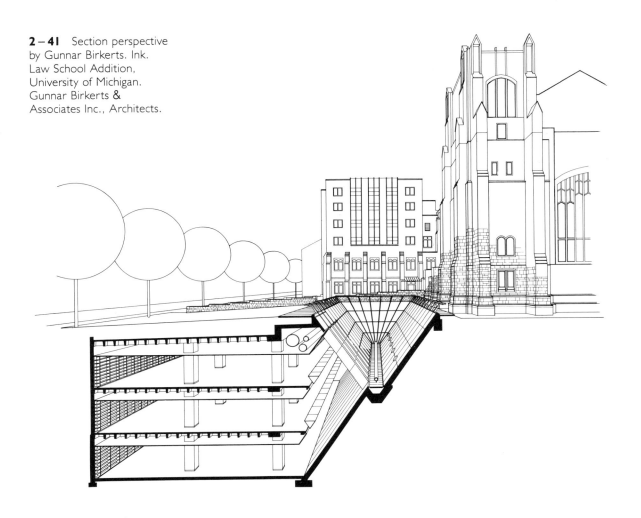

2 – 41 Section perspective
by Gunnar Birkerts. Ink.
Law School Addition,
University of Michigan.
Gunnar Birkerts &
Associates Inc., Architects.

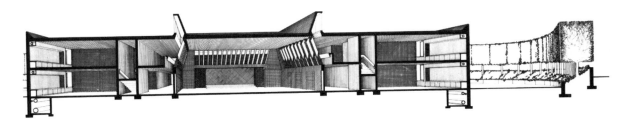

2 – 42 Section perspective
by Gunnar Birkerts. Ink.
Lincoln Elementary
School, Columbus, IN.
Gunnar Birkerts &
Associates Inc.

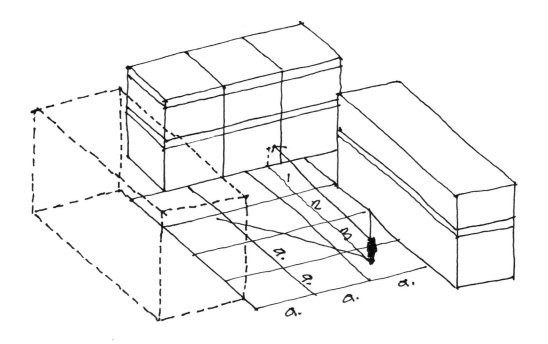

Depth In one-point perspective the sense of realism depends on a reasonably accurate depiction of depth. Skilled designers can sometimes make an accurate judgment of depth in a perspective; however, undisciplined use of the convention commonly leads to misrepresentations such as views of a space that would logically place the viewer outside of its walls.

Depth scaling in perspective is dependent upon the distance of the viewer from the object being viewed. There is a simple method of measuring perspective depth, by locating lines at forty-five-degree angles to the line of view both in plan and perspective. Using these forty-five-degree lines, we can draw like-scaled squares in perspective and plan so that any distance can be measured perpendicular to our view. We also can transfer an equal dimension from planes perpendicular to our line of view to planes parallel to our line of view.

2 – 43 through 2 – 45
One-point perspective constructions.

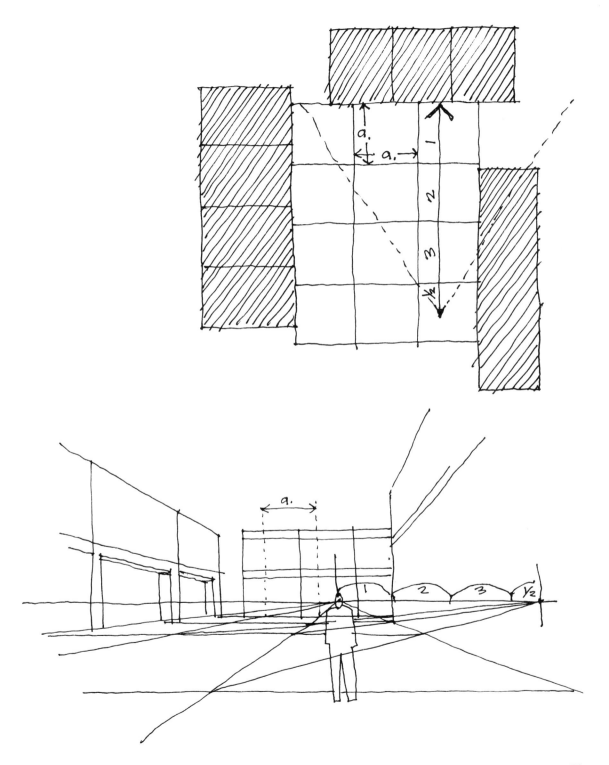

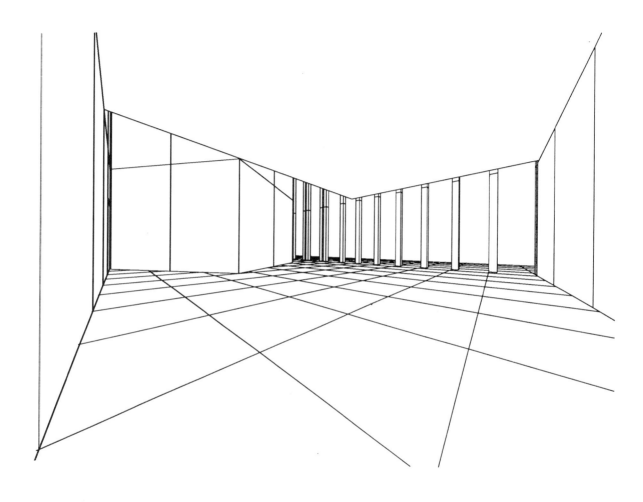

Distortion   Just as photographs of interior spaces taken with a wide-angle camera lens can make them look larger, distortions can be made in one-point perspective that lead us to see spaces either larger or smaller than reality. This is useful in some circumstances, but we should be careful not to deceive ourselves about the reality of the space nor to deceive the people for whom the space is being created. While one might take poetic license with drawing conventions for artistic or nonenvironmental reasons, it is best to build your perspective expertise on realistic use of the drawing convention.

2 – 46 through 2 – 48
Distorted perspectives. Computer graphic. Interior space studies.

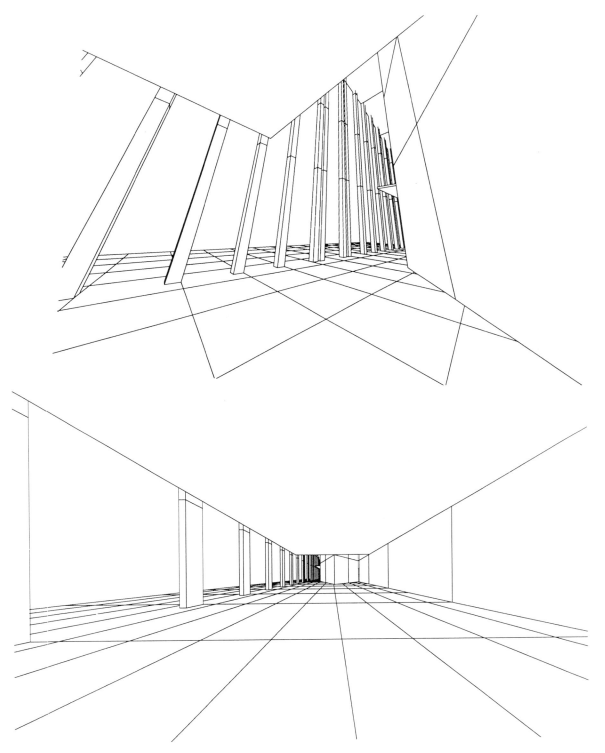

Modified One-point Perspective   One of the virtues of one-point perspective is its ease of construction within the area of a sheet of paper on which you are working. Modified one-point perspective, as developed by Kirby Lockard, combines the benefits of working within the area of a sheet of paper with the more realistic representation of a two-point perspective. As with a simple one-point perspective, the primary view is perpendicular to a surface; however, a modification, using a grid of consistently tapering lines, recognizes a second perspective point at a distance to either the left or right. The grid of tapering lines is constructed by establishing a constant distance between the lines at each edge of the paper. With the modified one-point perspective, we move away from the static view of the orthographic projection toward a sense of participation in the environment the drawing depicts. The perspective drawing should invite the client to participate in the experience of the environment. This is particularly important when you are involving clients in the design process.

2–49 through 2–51
Modified one-point perspectives by William Kirby Lockard. Felt pen.

2 – 52 Two-point
perspective by Koetter, Kim
& Associates, Inc. Ink. Class
of 1927/Clapp Hall,
Princeton University, NJ.
Koetter, Kim & Associates
Inc., Architects.

Two-point Perspective

If we only confronted environment as a series of planes approached
at a ninety-degree angle, one-point perspectives would suffice, but
because we regularly view environments at a variety of angles and
distances, the two-point perspective is a commonly used drawing
option. This convention is usually associated with exterior views of
objects or buildings, because the view of two or more sides provides a sense of their three-dimensional volume and composition.
Two-point perspective is also effective for looking at individual
spaces or multiple views along a route through a series of spaces.
Used properly, two-point perspectives can be very effective for
studying exterior public spaces.

Until recently, accurate two-point perspective was one of the
more complicated drawing conventions to construct and therefore
was little used as a study tool. With the advent of three-dimensional
computer-aided drawing programs, we should see more use of two-
point perspectives because of the relative ease with which they can
be generated. Some of these computer-aided programs facilitate
the study of design by allowing you to move rapidly from one convention to another (from section to plan to perspective) as you
develop or alter your design.

2 – 53 Two-point
perspective by Michael
Doyle. Felt pen. Lloyd
Center Food Court.
Communication Arts, Inc.,
Designer. Keeva Kekst,
Architect. Melvin Simon
& Associates, Project
Developer.

2 – 54 Two-point
perspective by Dick Sneary.
Technical pen on vellum.
Heartland Raceway, Topeka,
KS. Hellmuth Obata
Kassabaum, Architects.

Three-point Perspective

The bulk of our experience of space consists of views near or on a
horizontal plane. Consequently, for most studies of architectural
design, one-point or two-point perspectives will suffice. Occasionally,
however, when experience of spaces includes view lines on an acute
angle down or up, the three-point perspective is a useful convention. The three-point perspective is basically the same as the two-
point perspective, but a third point is added either above or below
the drawing to depict the experience of converging lines along the
vertical axis as well as the horizontal axis. In addition to showing the
experience of space, the three-point convention can help explain
the interrelationship of the parts of a building if important lines of
views are carefully selected.

2–55 Three-point interior
perspective by Paul
Stevenson Oles. Republic
Bank Tower Proposal,
Dallas, TX. Skidmore
Owings and Merrill-Chicago,
Architects.

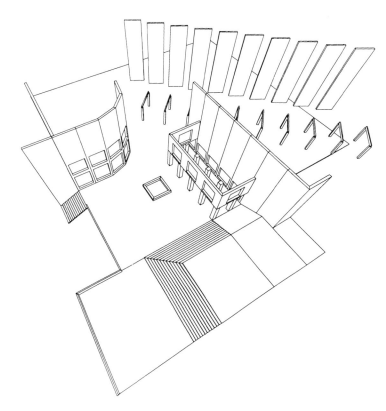

2 – 56 Three-point perspective by Paul Lew. Computer graphic. Public space study.

2 – 57 Three-point perspective. Felt pen. Urban Design Study, Athens, OH. Paul Laseau and Geoffrey Nishi, Architects.

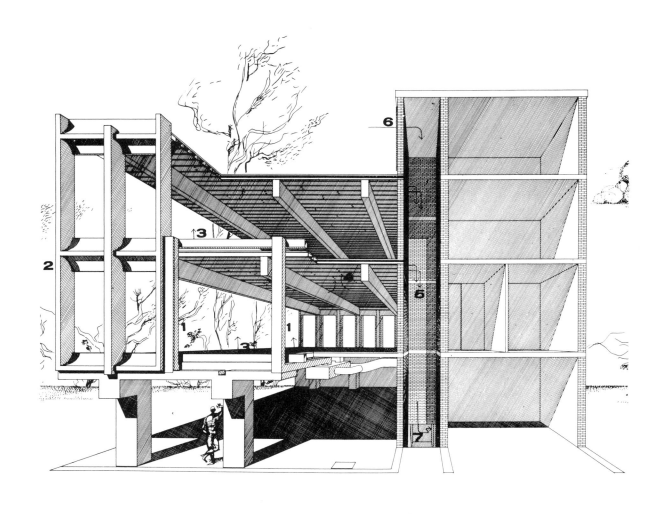

3 – 1 Disassembled perspective by Mitchell/Giurgola. Ink. American College of Life Underwriters Headquarters. Mitchell/Giurgola, Architects.

VIEW

3

Drawings of architecture are heavily influenced by the relationship between the viewer and the object being viewed. The angle and the direction of view fundamentally influence the experience represented by different drawing conventions. Views can also be narrowly exclusive or widely inclusive. Partial views draw attention to specific features and may also have an enticing power derived from the implied invitation to imagine those things that have been left out of the view. Conversely, Renaissance painters often took the broader, comprehensive view, including exterior and interior space and the foreground, middle ground, and background. These often contrived views provided a heightened awareness of the environmental context of the setting.

Selection of view is an important way to recognize the purpose and audience for the drawing. As designers, architects select views that adjust their own perceptions and provide a fresh view of the design work. A design team may assemble a wide array of views of a project to stimulate discussion and avoid overlooking important design issues. A carefully orchestrated set of views can help draw the client into the design discussions, adding a rich dimension to the process. View selection is particularly important for community or public audiences. Some views are easily understood while others may be confusing or threatening, discouraging participation in the design review.

3 – 2 Eye-level perspective by Dick Sneary. Felt pen. Cadman Yards Ballpark Warehouse, Baltimore, MD. Hellmuth Obata Kassabaum, Architects.

3 – 3 Eye-level perspective by Michael Doyle. Felt pen. Palm Court Study, Santa Monica Place, CA. Communication Arts, Inc., Designer. The Rouse Company, Project Developer.

3 – 4 Eye-level perspective by Hao-wei Yu. Ink. International Student Center Project, Ball State University, Muncie, IN.

EYE-LEVEL VIEW

Eye-level view is probably the most useful and practically informative angle of view because it represents the majority of our environmental experience and it helps the audience to place themselves in the proposed setting. The eye-level view also provides us with a baseline from which other features of a drawing can be understood, such as the scale and our relationship to people, spaces, and objects in the view. It helps us comprehend and evaluate the shapes and spaces being presented because we can relate it back to our own experience. When we ignore the utility of an eye-level view, we run the risk of throwing off or distorting perceptions of the environment, perceptions that are essential tools for design.

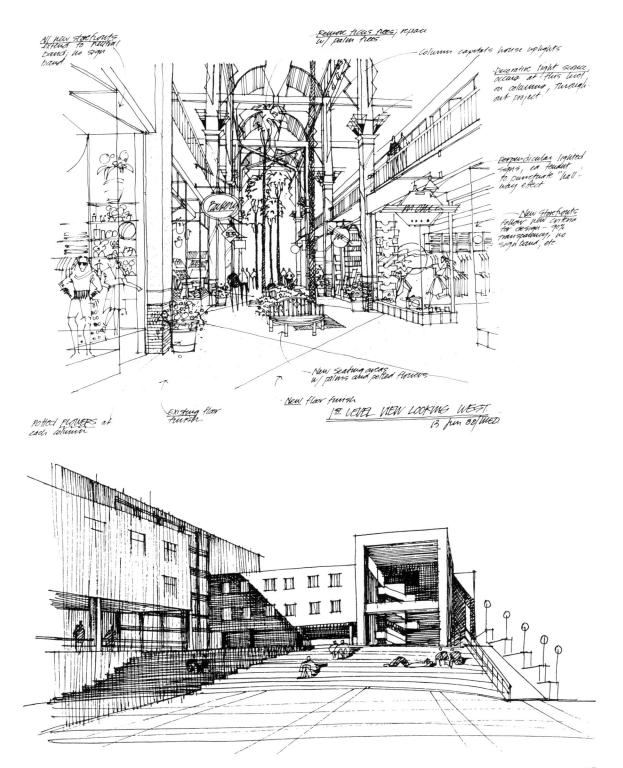

All new storefronts extend to neutral band; no sign band

Remove ficus trees; replace w/ palm trees.

Column capitals house uplights

Decorative light sconce, occurs at this level on columns, throughout project.

perpendicular lighted signs, ea tenant to punctuate "hallway effect

New storefronts follow new criteria for design — 90% transparency, no sign band, etc.

New seating areas w/ palms and potted flowers

Existing floor finish

New floor finish

1ST LEVEL VIEW LOOKING WEST
13 Jun 88/WED.

Potted FLOWERS at each column

65

3 – 5 Aerial view by Michael Reardon. Ink on mylar. San Francisco Waterfront Plan. ROMA Design Group.

AERIAL VIEW

Sometimes referred to as a bird's-eye view, this particular angle of view approximates our experience with miniature environments such as dollhouses or model train sets. For many people this is a comfortable, familiar orientation. Aerial views give us a comprehensive look at a total complex or a set of spaces so that we can understand the relationships while not losing the sense of their three-dimensionality. We can simultaneously understand the design concept and imagine the experience of being in the resulting spaces. Plan projections are often used interchangeably with this convention, providing the added advantage of being able to draw everything at a constant scale.

3 – 6 Aerial perspective by Hao-wei Yu. Ink. International Student Center Project, Ball State University, Muncie, IN.

3 – 7 Aerial view by Dick Sneary. Felt pen on marker paper. Poppy's Restaurant. Topsy's International, Inc.

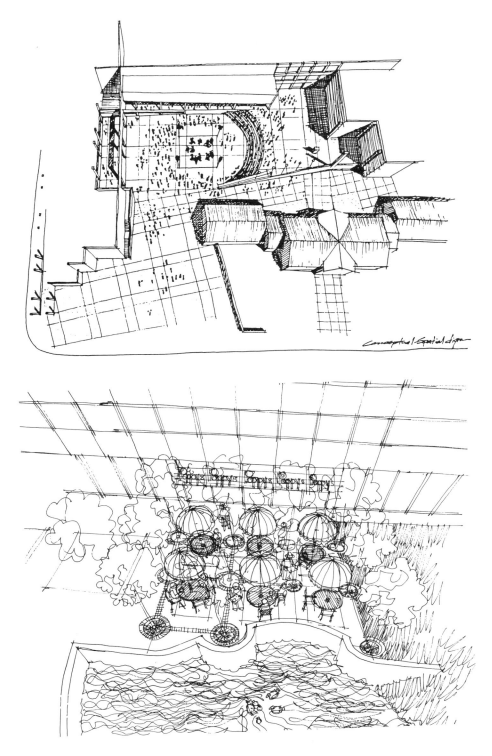

Conceptual Spatial diagram

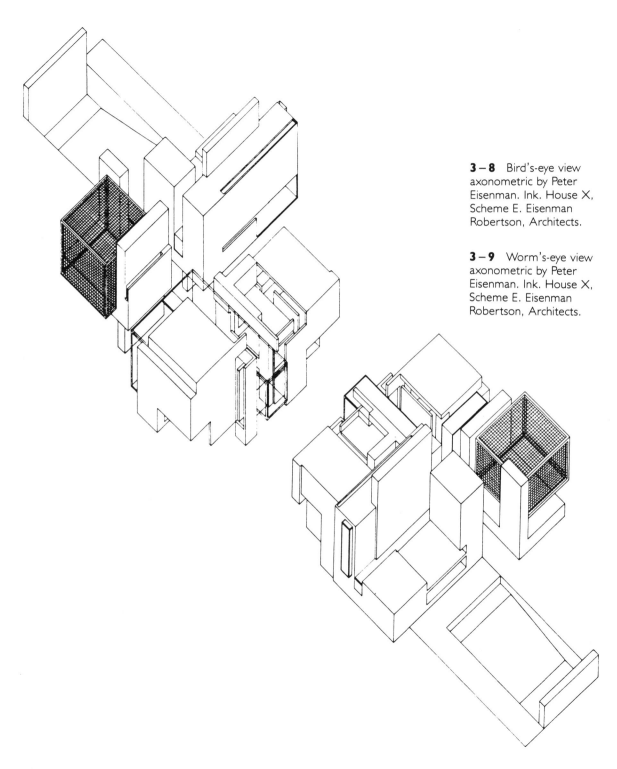

3 – 8 Bird's-eye view axonometric by Peter Eisenman. Ink. House X, Scheme E. Eisenman Robertson, Architects.

3 – 9 Worm's-eye view axonometric by Peter Eisenman. Ink. House X, Scheme E. Eisenman Robertson, Architects.

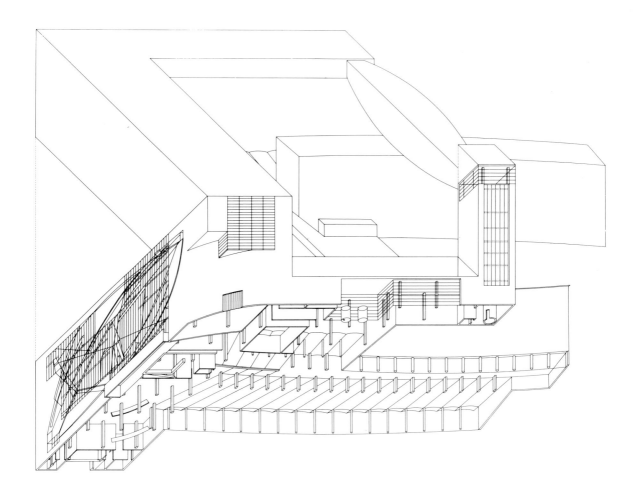

WORM'S-EYE VIEW

In many cases this view is produced by cutting a horizontal section through a building or space and then taking a view from the bottom. The upper portion of the view is rendered as either a paraline or perspective projection. While the worm's-eye view may be initially disorienting, it is particularly useful in showing the interior volume and detail of a space and also conveying a sense of its enclosure. Because of its unusual orientation, the worm's-eye view is also effective at promoting new conceptions of a design.

3 – 10 Worm's-eye view axonometric by Steven Holl. Ink. American Memorial Library, Berlin. Steven Holl, Architects.

69

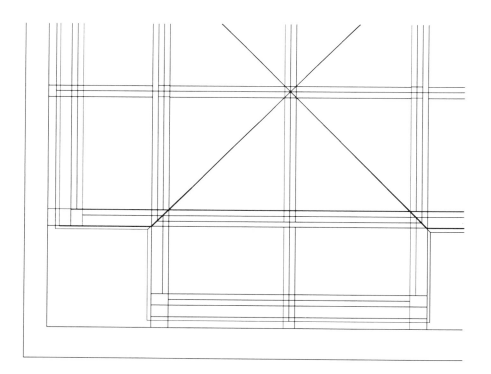

VIEW FRAMING

Often in the design process it is important to focus on particular parts of the building to the exclusion of others, to concentrate on a more detailed composition or refinement. Partial plans, sections, or elevations are commonly used in design development when studying facade detail and composition. One might draw a wall section and partial exterior and interior elevations to reveal their relationships to each other and study the integration of various systems in the exterior enclosure wall. Traditionally, beginning with early architectural drawings and extending to those produced in recent times in some offices, partial sections and elevations were rendered at full scale. This increasingly rare practice may be revived because of computer-aided drawing. It is now possible to draw a partial section or elevation at a smaller scale on a computer and then print a copy of the enlarged drawing at full scale. The ease with which these drawings can be made and manipulated may reinstate a common practice of viewing parts of a building at full scale as part of design development. They may also foster a return of interest in ornament and more elaborate detail in buildings, since the ability to easily draw complicated detail or ornament promotes its inclusion in design development.

3 – 11 Partial section by Kevin Forseth. Computer graphic (Architrion). House III.

3 – 12 Partial perspective by Kevin Forseth. Computer graphic (Architrion). House III.

3 – 13 Partial plan by Kevin Forseth. Computer graphic (Architrion). House III.

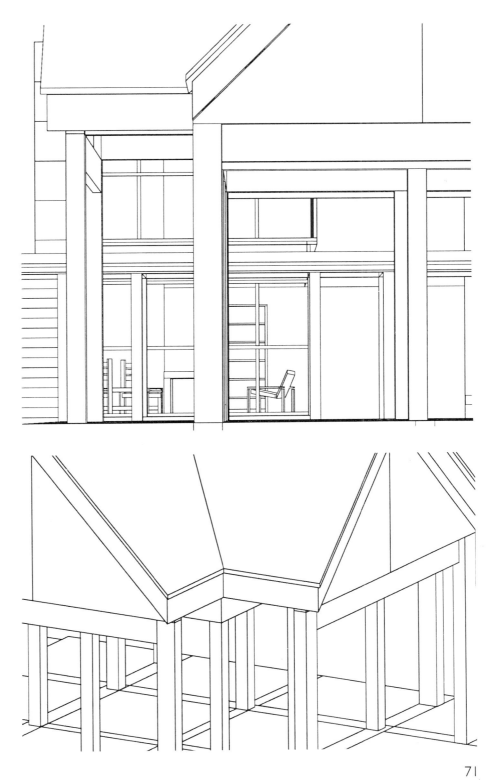

3 – 14   Vignette sketch.

VIGNETTES

This type of drawing produces what one might call a soft frame. The essential part of the drawing is rendered at the center with much detail and information, whereas, increasingly less detail is provided as the edge of the drawing is approached. This produces a fuzzy, out-of-focus image toward the drawing edges, simulating the sensation of peripheral vision. The vignette is most commonly used in perspective projections, but it could be applied to other conventions as well. One of the features of the vignette is the suggested extension of a clearly focused view in directions away from the drawing, leaving to the viewer's imagination the creation of the rest of the environment.

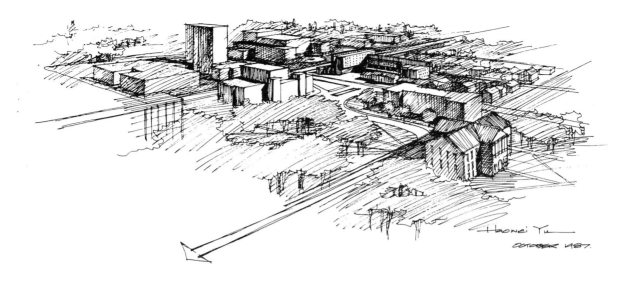

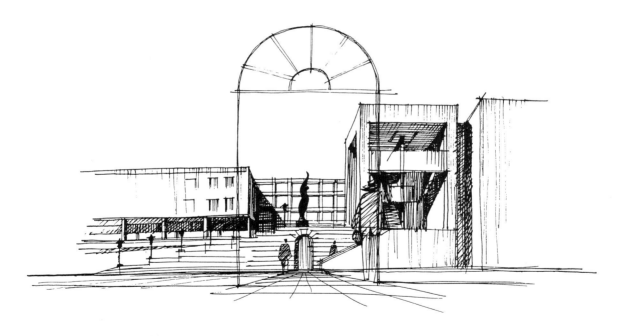

3 – 15 and 3 – 16
Vignette sketches by
Hao-wei Yu. Ink.
International Student Center
Project, Ball State University,
Muncie, IN.

VIEW COMBINATIONS

Traditionally the principal use of drawings by architects has been to represent the experience and composition of two-dimensional planes or three-dimensional space. But spatial experience has a fourth dimension—time. Our kinesthetic experience of a building is not captured in a single view, but in the combination of several views accumulated as we move through space. One way designers capture this experience is by creating serial views, a series of sketch perspectives taken at various points along a path through an environment. When displayed as a sequence, these drawings help the viewer create the sensation of actually being in the environment. In recent years serial perspectives have been generated by moving a video camera through a model at eye level and then pulling the individual images from the videotape for use as the basis for the perspectives.

3

ΟΔΟΣ ΔΗΛΟΥ
ΜΥΚΟΝΟΣ
GREECE
20 APRIL 82

3 – 17 through 3 – 20

Analysis plans of progression through a street in Mykonos by Steven House. Felt pen on Strathmore. Studies for Mediterranean Indigenous Architecture Exhibition. House + House, Architects, San Francisco.

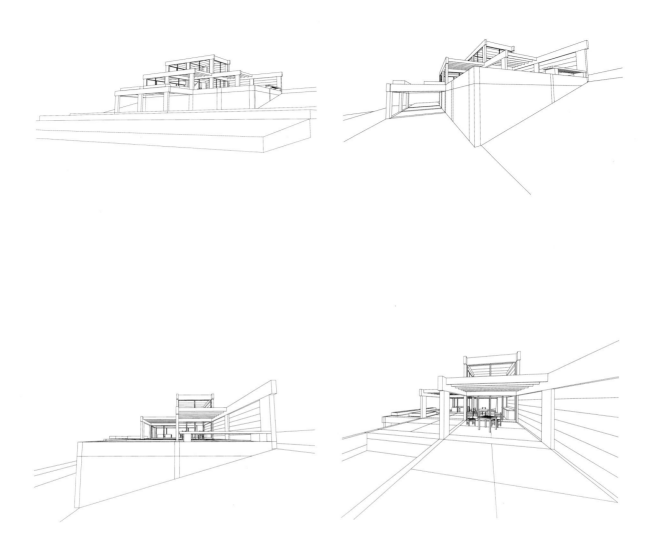

With the advent of three-dimensional computer graphics, we can now lay out a path of movement through a space, establishing the position and direction of views, and automatically generate a perspective series. This ability, possibly more than any other of computer graphics, may revolutionize the way in which we use drawings to study design and thereby alter the sensitivities, criteria, and qualities that apply to architectural design.

76

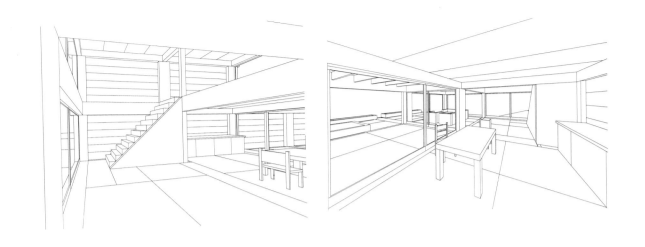

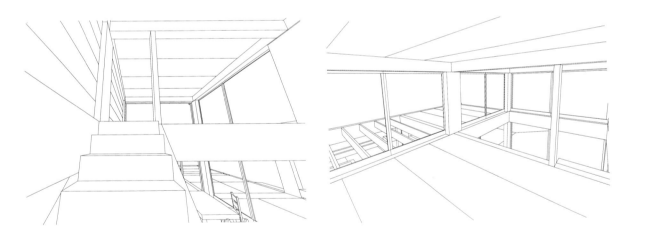

3 – 21 through 3 – 28
Perspective series by Kevin
Forseth. Computer graphic
(Architrion). House II.

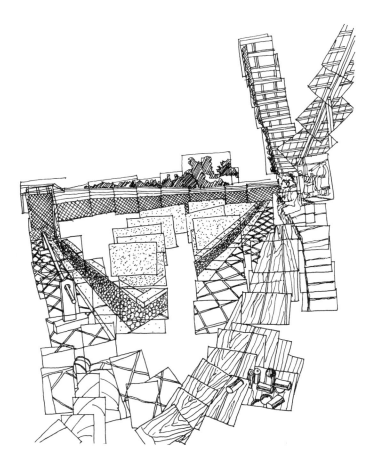

3 – 29 Composite view, based on photographic montage by David Hockney, by Paul Lew. Felt pen. Kyoto Temple Garden, Japan.

COMPOSITE AND SIMULTANEOUS VIEWS

This approach to drawing varies from serial views in that it does not attempt to present a realistic sequence of view as one moves through a space Instead, composite and simultaneous views combine in one drawing several different views of an environment at various scales, providing a general impression of its aesthetic experience. David Hockney's photographic work is a fine example of the potential of composite views. In addition to shifts in scale, he uses repetition of view fragments to intensify the experience. Experiments by the cubist school of painting provide an approach to representing the fourth dimension, time, which might be useful in design. The cubists simultaneously layered different views of a subject, integrating multiple views of a subject in one drawing. These techniques for representing experience can help the designer break away from staid perceptions that may result from more standard drawing conventions, inviting the use of abstraction and the exploration of meaning.

3 – 30 Composite drawing by Morphosis. Ink. Sixth Street House. Morphosis, Architects.

3 – 31 Composite drawing by Paul Lew. Computer graphic. Mystery House Studies. Paul Laseau, Architect.

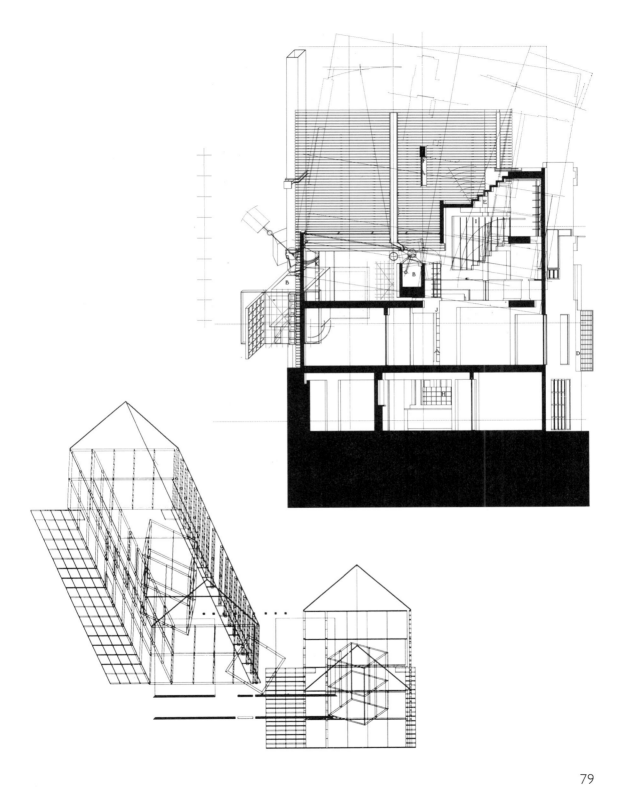

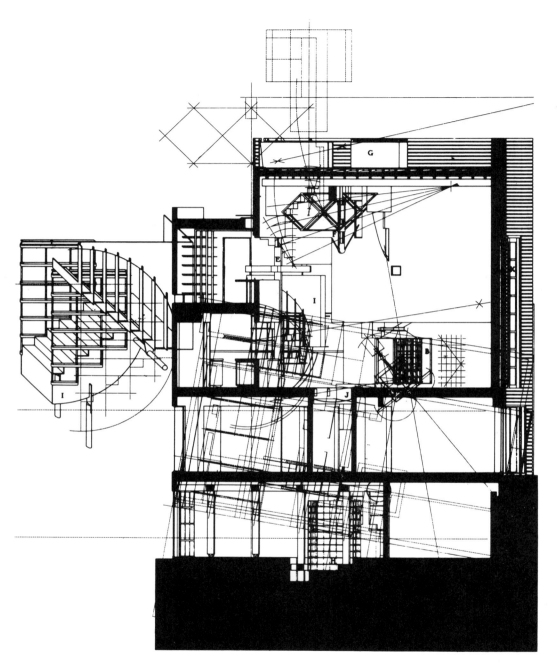

3 – 32 and 3 – 33
Simultaneous views by
Morphosis. Ink. Sixth Street
House. Morphosis,
Architects.

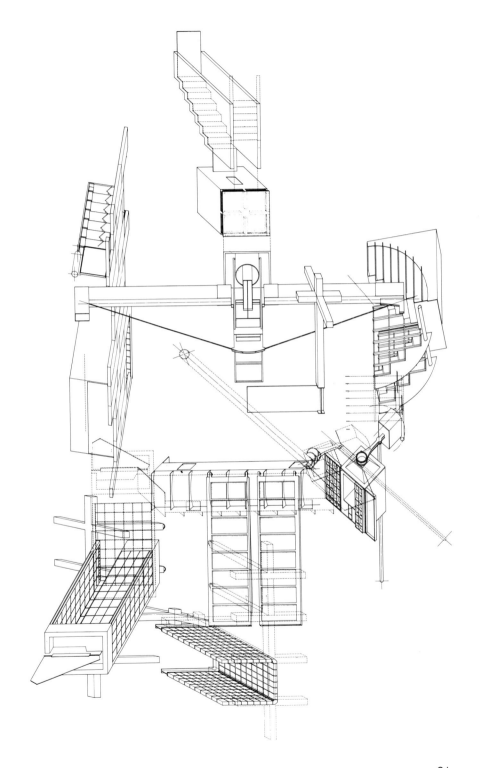

81

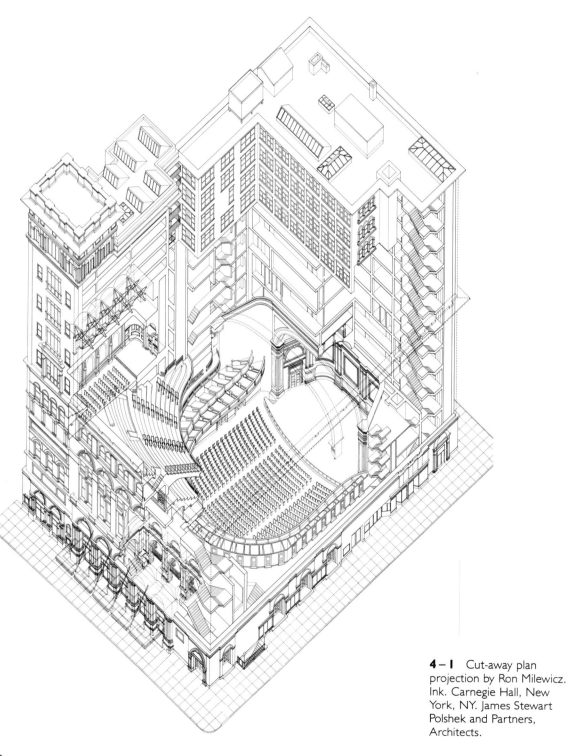

4 – 1 Cut-away plan projection by Ron Milewicz. Ink. Carnegie Hall, New York, NY. James Stewart Polshek and Partners, Architects.

SUBJECT

4

One of the most significant and interesting distinctions between photography and drawing is the ability to edit freely in drawing. A designer has the ability to eliminate or transform all or portions of the subject of the drawing and create views that would be impossible to achieve with a camera. This editing capability is not artificial or irrelevant; it is identical to our normal visual experience. Our eyes are constantly bombarded with images to which they must constantly adjust in order to take in an incredible amount of information. To cope with all this information, from early childhood we develop the ability to be selective. As babies we are able to focus on only those things that are close at hand; slowly, as we learn to cope with our visual environment, we also develop the ability to focus on objects increasingly distant from us. As we grow older we develop a selective visual attention to those things that are important to us, whether for purposes of safety or efficiency. We tend to focus on people's faces, on anything moving rapidly in our peripheral view that might be threatening, on the ground if it feels hazardous, or on signs as we drive. As we grow up, we integrate these tendencies in the form of perceptions that act like sorting machines, making us more aware of some parts of our visual experience.

As designers we can consciously manipulate those perceptions and properly focus them for the task as hand. The subject we choose for a drawing can be a means of selecting the perceptual focus we want to use. Stripping away parts of a building subject can emphasize the form and expression of interior spaces and their relationship to the exterior form. Pulling the subject apart may reveal the underlying conceptual organization of a design. In a drawing we can make parts of a subject transparent or invisible, to support insight and understanding.

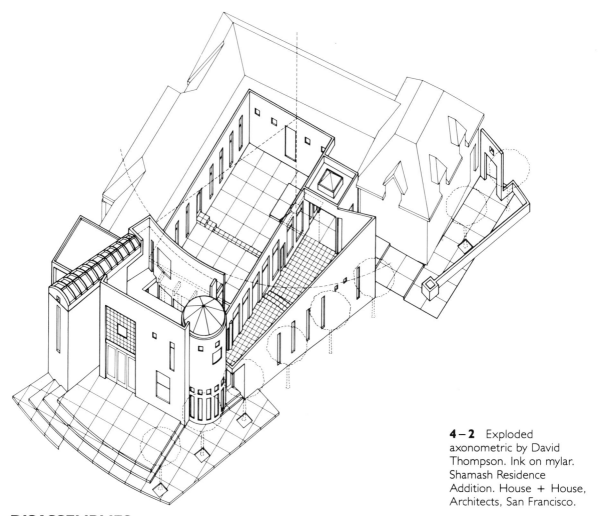

4 – 2 Exploded axonometric by David Thompson. Ink on mylar. Shamash Residence Addition. House + House, Architects, San Francisco.

DISASSEMBLIES

In this approach to drawing, the subject is treated as if it were a model that can be taken apart so that different parts may be examined. In a disassembly we cut portions out of surfaces or remove walls, floors, or roofs of buildings so that we can view the interior. This approach is most commonly used in paraline projection drawings but has also been used effectively in perspective projections. Variations on this type of drawing range from opening up the sides of one particular space or removing the roof to taking whole sections of a building away in order to see into other parts. Traditionally, creating disassembly drawings has been very time consuming, but the developments in computer graphic modeling are reducing the effort required to produce them, making them much more accessible for designing.

4 – 3 Disassembled
paraline projection by
Richard Meier. Ink.
Dormitory for Olivetti
Training Center, Tarrytown,
NY. Richard Meier &
Partners, Architects.

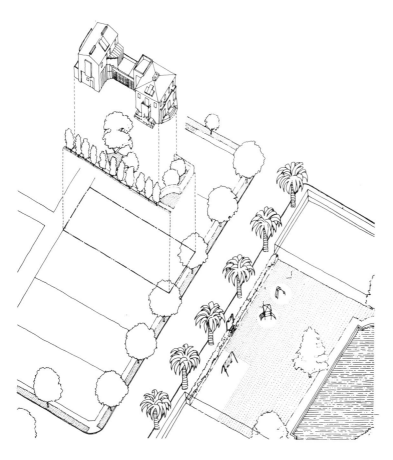

4 – 4 Exploded view by Koning Eizenberg. California Avenue Duplex, Santa Monica, CA. Koning Eizenberg Architecture.

EXPLODAMETRICS

This is an improvised term for a drawing in which the subject has the appearance of being blown apart into several pieces. Using a three-dimensional drawing convention, components such as walls, floors, ceilings, windows, panels, or furniture are disconnected and moved away from the center of the drawing and each other, clearly revealing the components and their relationships. To assist the viewer in understanding the way in which the parts were originally connected, dotted lines are commonly used to represent the paths along which the objects have moved in the process of disconnecting. Although moving the disconnected parts on orthogonal paths usually produces the clearest drawing, it is sometimes an advantage to use a curved or irregular path of movement. The explodametric has been explored to some extent as a result of the deconstructivist movement. It will probably be explored even further as we find these drawing manipulation capabilities more readily available through the use of three-dimensional computer graphics.

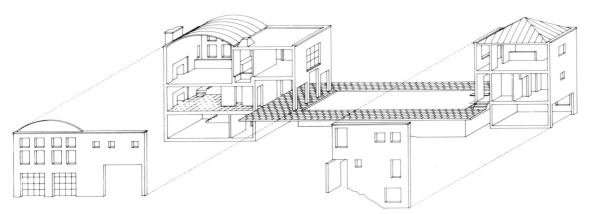

4 – 5 Cutaway elevation
and section by Steven Holl.
Ink. Van Zandt Residence.
Steven Holl, Architects.

4 – 6 Explodametric
drawing by Jim Stutzman.
Computer graphic
(Architrion). MuseHouse.
Stutzman & Associates,
Architects.

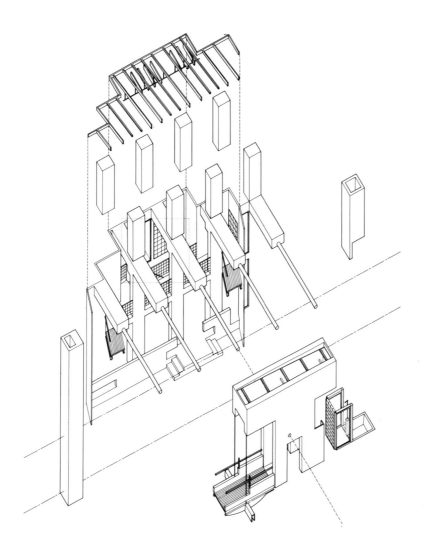

4 – 7 Paraline projection with selected details by Morphosis. Ink. Malibu Beach House, CA. Morphosis, Architects.

SELECTION

A highly useful variation of subject manipulation is the selective representation of design components that remain in their original relationship to each other. This creates the impression that these pieces are floating in space without the intervening elements. The exposed components can be clearly rendered in considerable detail while retaining a general sense of the context in which they fit. One form of these drawings shows layers of planes in either plan or elevation, emphasizing the conceptual basis for sequences of spaces or continuities of form. Another practical application of selection is the illustration of the assembly sequence for detailed component design, such as cabinetry.

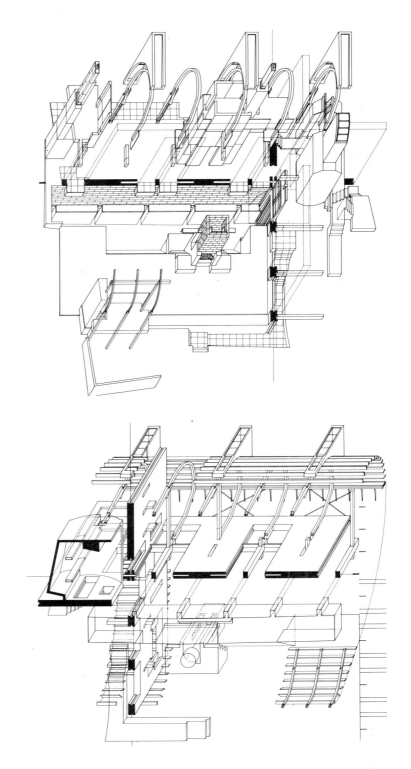

4 – 8 and 4 – 9 Layered drawings by Morphosis. Ink. Reno House. Morphosis, Architects.

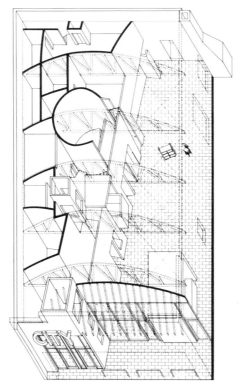

4 – 10 Transparent view by Schweitzer/Kellen, Inc. City Restaurant. Schweitzer/Kellen, Architects.

TRANSPARENCY

In addition to editing parts of a subject, we can transform the parts by making them appear transparent. These drawings are useful for understanding the relationship between spaces, between the exterior and the interior of a building, or between the form of the enclosure and the configuration of space. Transparent components are often indicated with dotted outlines of their profiles. In three-dimensional drawings views are carefully selected to reveal clearly both transparent and visible parts of the subject. Transparency is also useful in conceptual drawings as a way to suggest the interaction of spaces or activities.

Another type of transparency represents what we cannot see in the form of dotted ghosts, so that we are aware of their relationship to those objects we can see. Ghost images may depict elements on the far side of a wall or they can represent objects behind the viewer. For some purposes we might combine both the disassembly and transparency techniques to achieve the clearest understanding of the subject. Caution should be taken to avoid manipulating objects just to make spectacular drawings; rather, the technique should clarify understanding or experiences of the designed environment.

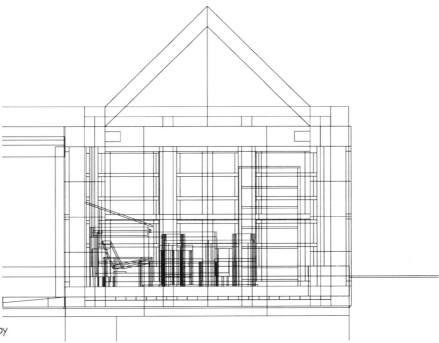

4 – 11 Transparent view by
Kevin Forseth. Computer
graphic. House III.

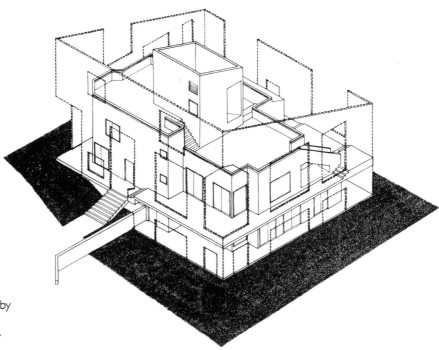

4 – 12 Transparent view by
MTLW, Architects. Ink.
Zimmerman House, 1975.
MTLW, Architects.

SETTING

5

5 – 1 Exterior perspective, day view, by Paul Stevenson Oles. Black Prismacolor on Strathmore board. Louvre Museum Addition, Paris. I. M. Pei and Partners, Architects.

5 – 2 Exterior perspective, night view, by Paul Stevenson Oles. White Prismacolor on black museum board. Louvre Museum Addition, Paris. I. M. Pei and Partners, Architects.

Every design project exists within some context that influences our experience and understanding of what we design. Built environments appear differently in different climates and lighting conditions, in the morning, afternoon, evening, or night and in different seasons of the year. Architects must be aware of the context in which their designs are developed in order to integrate them within that context. By studying the climatic and other effects of a setting on the building, the architect can explore the full range of experiences and conditions that people will encounter as they use the building. Drawings can be used to project the possible changes in appearance of the building and to illustrate the experience of the setting that one can have from within a space or building. These experiences and surroundings become part of the total experience of the designed environment. For example, the criteria for size, shape, and position of windows is not only a function of the light and the air to be let into spaces but also of the desired views through windows to the surrounding site.

Designers are often tempted to simply focus on the design of buildings, without any effective awareness of context. This can lead to self-centered architecture that does not contribute to the definition of exterior spaces. If we are to improve the quality of shared public space, designers must purposely study context as well as buildings. To include context in design studies, the scope and content of design drawings must include a view of impacts of the building setting.

LIGHT

Only through the existence of light and its antithesis, darkness, can
we visually experience environment. Through the action of light and
shadow, by association with other senses, we perceive shape, con-
tour, texture, composition, scale, heat, cold. The movement of the
sun daily and at different seasons of the year animates environments. All of the views that we have discussed so far, whether elevation or perspective, take on a new sense of realism with the
rendering of shade and shadow. Steve Oles's faithfully realistic
approach to architectural illustration relies primarily on the rendition
of all the values between light and darkness caused by the action of
light upon a space or volume. He has had a significant influence in
stimulating the architectural community to a new awareness of the
role of light in architectural design, as the many drawings he has
contributed to this chapter will reveal. His sketch studies of the East
Wing of the National Gallery show the basic effectiveness of this
approach. Through these drawings we are able to study space in its
fundamental configuration, within the context of light.

5 – 3 Exterior perspective
by Paul Stevenson Oles.
Black Prismacolor on
laminated vellum. Johnson &
Johnson Headquarters, New
Brunswick, NJ. I. M. Pei and
Partners, Architects.

94

5 – 4 through 5 – 6
Interior perspective studies
by Paul Stevenson Oles.
Black Prismacolor on tracing
paper. National Gallery of
Art, East Building,
Washington, DC. I. M. Pei
and Partners, Architects.

5 – 7 Study of reflections by Paul Stevenson Oles. Black Prismacolor on laminated vellum. Dallas Centre Development, Dallas, TX. I. M. Pei and Partners, Architects.

Reflections are an important dimension of light. Because of the traditional difficulty of accurately rendering reflections, they are often omitted or represented symbolically. Yet reflective surfaces often play a central role in the experience of architecture and its setting. The reflection of trees in a glass building facade doubles the impact of the natural setting. Reflections also contribute a desirable level of complexity to the experience of environment. Careful rendering of reflections provides a more realistic perception of glazed or polished surfaces or environmental features such as water.

5 – 8 Study of reflections by Paul Stevenson Oles. Black Prismacolor on laminated vellum. Austral Lineas Aereas Headquarters Proposal. I. M. Pei and Partners, Architects.

5 – 9 Study of reflections by Paul Stevenson Oles. Black Prismacolor and graphite on tracing paper. Glover's Landing, Marblehead, MA. Allan Chapman Associates, Inc., Architects.

5 – 10 Exterior perspective, night view, by Paul Stevenson Oles. White Prismacolor on black museum board. U.S. Holocaust Memorial Museum. Notter, Finegold & Alexander, Architects.

5 – 11 Exterior perspective, night view, by Paul Stevenson Oles. White Prismacolor on black museum board. Jacob K. Javits Convention Center, New York, NY. I. M. Pei and Partners, Architects.

Another dimension of light is the action of artificial light. Much of our experience of buildings is that of enclosed space, and it is largely because of artificial lighting that we receive impressions of that space. The experience of some interior spaces is totally determined by the pattern and color of lights. In restaurant design, lighting is often vital to the definition and mood of spaces. The interior lighting of a building, particularly at night, significantly affects the exterior appearance of buildings and the public spaces they help define. Designers can use drawings to evaluate the impact of different positioning and intensities of lighting as part of the design decisions for a building. While depiction of lighting has usually been delegated to the illustrator or model builder, in the future computer graphics should also put this ability in the hands of the designer.

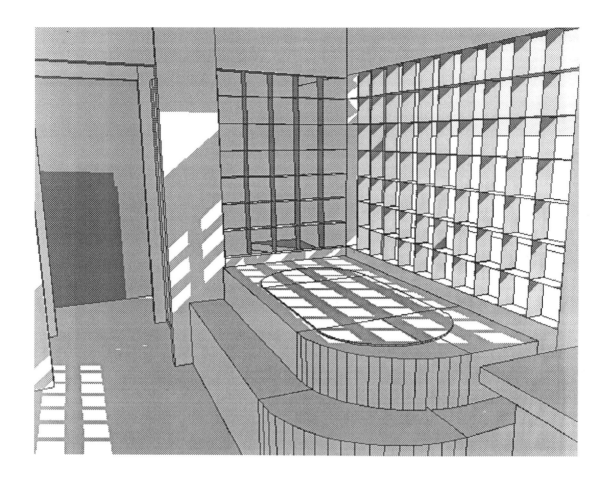

The interaction of sunlight and structure plays a major role in the perceived aesthetics of a design. Although many architects will use shadow-rendered facade studies in the course of design, comprehensive studies of the effects of sunlight have usually been considered a luxury. This view is about to change. Computer graphic programs are being developed that replicate the action of the sun at different times of the year or day. Some animated programs can simulate the action of the sun over a period of time. Soon appropriate studies of the interaction of sunlight, and of artificial light, on the appearance and experience of architecture will be a practical option. But designers must develop a corresponding awareness and concern for the impact of light if these tools are to benefit the design process.

5 – 12 through 5 – 14
Interior perspectives by Lee Anderson. Computer graphic (Space Maker). University of Minnesota, Department of Architecture.

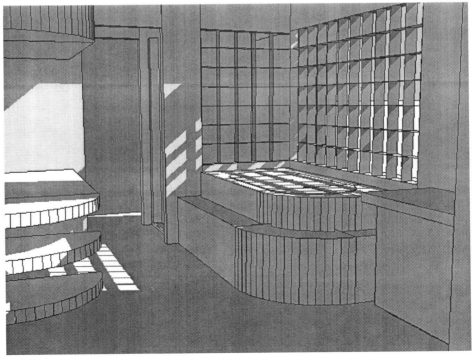

ATMOSPHERE

Spatial experience of environment is also influenced by the surrounding atmosphere. Distant objects may seem less focused and less intensely colored. On overcast days buildings exhibit softer, more subtle values. Warm colors—red, yellow, and orange—appear more vibrant in southern exposures, while cool colors—green and blue—appear more intense in north light. At certain times of the day, particularly at sunrise and sunset, the bending of light in the atmosphere can paint the surfaces of a building with a dazzling array of colors. Depictions of these different conditions become part of the task of representation in studying an architectural design because they are a legitimate part of the day-to-day experience of the constructed environment.

5 – 15 Rendering by Richard Lovelace. Charcoal pencil on tracing paper. New York West Waterfront International Competition. Richard Lovelace, Architect.

5 – 16 Atmospheric drawing by Octavio Figueroa. Pencil on tracing paper. New York Hilton Addition Competition. The Eggars Group.

5 – 17 Rendering by Michael Elavsky. Ink on mylar. CONAGRA Corporate Headquarters. Opus Corporation, Architects.

5 – 18 Rendering by James Hadley. Nylon-tipped pen. Round Hill Estate, Nevis, West Indies. Gaudy-Hadley Associates, Architects.

5 – 19 Rendering by David M. Lane. Pen and ink on mylar, marker, and watercolor. The Base, Telluride, CO. Wheeler, Piper, Architects.

CONTEXT

There is an Oriental philosophy stating that the essence of the visible is that which you cannot see—translated into practical, visual terms, the perceived qualities of an object or building are heavily influenced by the qualities of the immediate context. Elementary color theory explains a comparable effect as dynamic contrast. Painters know that you can increase the intensity of a color by surrounding it with a color of contrasting hue or value or of decreased intensity. In representing architectural design, we must be equally aware of the qualities of the surroundings and the elements we are designing. To draw a building as an independent object when it will be located in a forest ignores a fundamental condition for experiencing the qualities that the building will have.

5 – 20 through 5 – 22
Perspective sketches. Felt
pen. Unity Temple. Frank
Lloyd Wright, Architect.

Another way to understand the influence of context is as
sequence. The sense of quiet and peace of a garden may be intensi-
fied if experienced as the conclusion of a transition from a busy
urban street. In many of Frank Lloyd Wright's buildings, he leads
you through an entry sequence of constrained low-ceiling passages
in preparation for the dramatic experience of the large central
space. The deprivation of the comparatively small, dark spaces sets
you up for the exhilarating effect of the central space. As designers,
then, we must include in our repertoire design drawings that reveal
the context as well as the design subject.

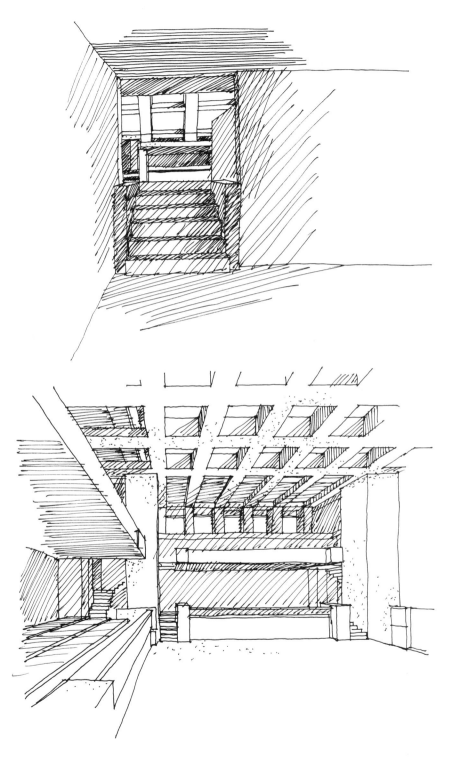

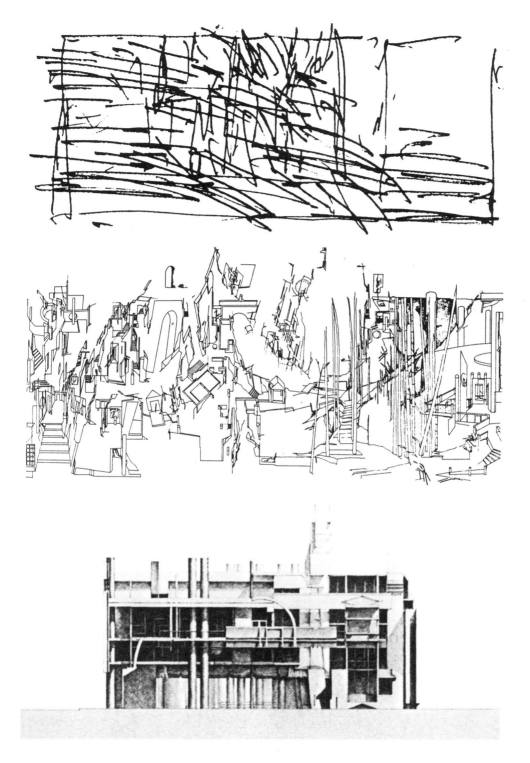

MEDIUM 6

Other important drawing options lie in the selection of the medium through which we communicate. Today's designer has the benefit of a rich array of media with which to communicate to himself and to others. Important variables in media include:

- The channel through which we communicate, from traditional exhibit or presentation to more advanced video/computer presentations
- The instruments we use within those channels, such as ink, pencil, or electronic color
- Features such as size, composition, definition, and distortion
- The style with which we communicate, which is often personal, conveying special qualities of our brand of design thinking.

Architectural designers tend to adopt media they find comfortable, those that can form a symbiotic relationship with their concerns and pattern of thinking about architecture. An architect who is heavily concerned with the experience of moving through an environment will use serial perspectives as a design study tool; another architect with a strong interest in the clarity and definition of volumetric composition in light will use models or rendered isometric drawings.

Personal choices about media are often altered to meet the needs of the intended audience. Designers must constantly remind themselves that drawings are communication tools and that there are media that are appropriate for communicating with themselves and other media appropriate for communicating with other professionals or clients, depending on the situation. Designers particularly need to keep in mind that communication with a client is not simply presenting their ideas but establishing a dialogue with the client in which a free exchange of ideas can take place.

6 – 1 Sketch study as a source for ideas by Jerry Exline. Pen and ink.

6 – 2 Design sketch by Yim Chan. Ink. A Temple for Lao Tzu, from *Carleton Book*, Carleton University, School of Architecture, 1986.

6 – 3 Rendering by Dwight Lander. Pencil. Granville Townsite, from *Carleton Book*, Carleton University, School of Architecture, 1986.

Different architectures will crown the islands since the city as collective work of art is built up by different generations and individuals.

ur Corbusier's 'open hand' will be relocated close to Chelsea Piers at the north end of the site, welcoming people from everywhere.

The island as recreation center

Pier 42 is the proposed location for a new city hall surrounded by a gathering plaza which continues across Westside Boulevard.

CHANNELS OF COMMUNICATION
Mounted Presentations

The traditional formal channel of communication with clients has been the mounted presentation. The principal advantage of this medium is that several drawings can be viewed and shared with a large audience, allowing review and selective focus on a particular drawing while retaining the context of the other drawings. This approach is also used for peer reviews of design projects where the design team is taking a critical view of the project and developing responses to the issues being raised by the discussion. The mounted presentation is not often used by the individual designer to communicate with himself, although it may be an appropriate option in some situations. Usually designers do their thinking in the midst of small sketches scattered around their desk or temporarily mounted on the wall. These sketches are often accompanied by study models.

Architects who are increasingly concerned about the amount of time and manpower spent preparing mounted presentations have begun to explore alternative media. Architectural firms should carefully review the purposes and objectives of and approaches to communication at all levels and experiment with alternative methods that will consume less of their valuable design time and resources.

6 – 4 and 6 – 5
Design presentation by Carlos Casuscelli and Michel Mounayar. Ink and marker on vellum. New York West Waterfront International Competition.

6 – 6 Design study sketches by Carlos Casuscelli and Michel Mounayar. Felt pen. New York West Waterfront International Competition.

Sections

Interior courts and gardens

City boulevard relationship

Contact with waterfront is multiplied by doubling the walkway and the sense of water is reinforced.

two major parallel walkways are proposed extending the full lenght of the site.One faces the river and the other further inland is intimate in scale.

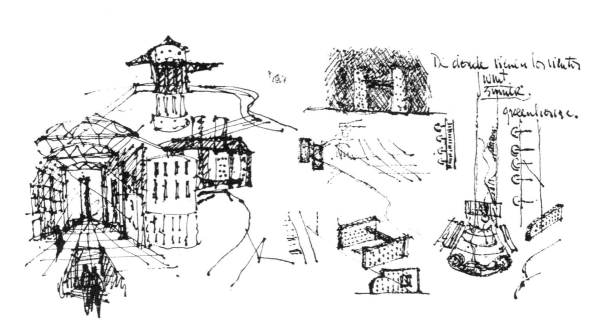

Townscape

Access - a point where you enter, a space of arrival or approach, like a front door.
Barrier - a natural or man-made obstacle that obstructs passage, view, sound: railroad or hedge.
Buffer - an element which softens differences between two conflicting activity areas.
Bypass - a special traffic route around the town.
Central business district - C.B.D. - the city's central concentrated area of business/commercial and cultural facilities, downtown.
Cluster - a group of similar and/or dissimilar buildings sharing a common territory and facilities.
Cohesiveness - a similarity between elements which promotes a common identity.
Commercial strip - a linear, automobile-oriented, commercial route.
Constraint - something you can't change (existing or potential).
Courthouse square - the block in which the courthouse is located. The principle public meeting place and facility in the county.
District - a defined area of the city that has a common identifying character throughout, CBD., industrial.
Edge - linear element not considered a path; often forms boundaries, blocking cross movement.
Element - an object or set of objects which form an identifiable part of an environment, a tree, a row of buildings, a park.
Focal point - a central object that attracts attention.

Focus - to give importance to a physical object or space.
Grid - a uniformly spaced network of roads lying parallel and perpendicular to each other.
Image - the perception that people have of an area of the city through experience, hearing about it, reading about it, etc.
Landmark - prominent or conspicuous object or building in the town that serves as a guide.
Land use - common use of an area of land: residential, commercial, industrial, etc.
Node - a spot in a city which normally is thought of as a center of activity.
Opportunity - any positive condition (existing or potential).
Path - a route, course or track along which movement occurs; street.
Pattern - a relative order of purposeful relationships, a consistent relationship of elements.
Place - a physical setting having a particular function, character, and form which may be occupied continuously or occasionally by people.
Subdivision - a separate land tract of housing.
Town entry - a place where one enters the town - gateway.
Town square - the major public open meeting place.
View - sight observed from one point.
Visual order - observable harmony between similar and dissimilar elements.

- Commercial
- Industrial
- Residential
- Recreational
- Institutional

6 Land Use Diagram   Open Space Plan

Shelbyville Tenn. Plan

diagram

Philadelphia plan

diagram

Reports

The increasing diversity of clients, each with their own internal communication needs or preferences, has made the illustrated report a popular alternative to the mounted design presentation. Some architectural firms believe that they are not producers of drawings or contract documents but are more accurately described as being in the business of publishing drawings and specifications for projects. This reflects a new attitude toward the use of media and methods of communicating, resulting in new concerns. The degree of reduction required for many drawings intended for reports requires the original drawings to have clear separations between lines and controlled value densities that produce readable drawings at a reduced scale. Another important consideration for the report format is sequential structure. To achieve simultaneous access to different levels of information similar to that found in a mounted presentation, a clear hierarchy within the report must be created graphically. Reports must be designed with the same care as any visual presentation.

6 – 7 Illustrated report by Harry Eggink. Ink on vellum. From *Urban Design Dictionary: Small Town Central District*. Harry Eggink, Ball State University, Muncie, IN.

112

Central District

Activity generator - a facility that acts as a focal point for activity and events.
Alley - a mid-block path or service route.
Building use - the way a building responds to usage: zoning, entry, character.
Bulkhead - a small structure on the roof which allows for roof access.
Circulation - pattern of movement for vehicles, services, pedestrians, public transportation, etc.
Historic focus - common historical style of a district: Victorian, Federal, Colonial.
Infrastructure - the basic organization systems of the city: streets, utilities, etc.
Interface - the process of meeting, connecting two elements, ideas, etc.
Organizing element - the basic man-made or natural form that organizes the town's form: courthouse, river, railroad, etc.
Parking - storage area for vehicles.
  Short term - a short time period for parking
  Long term - a long time period for parking
Public space - an area which is accessible to the public.
Public transportation - transportation available for public use.
Sense of place - having an awareness of location or physical environment.
Streetscape - the corridor of space bounded by the facades of the buildings on either side of the street, set of elements which form a street corridor or sit within that corridor: facades, pavement, trees, street lamps, traffic lights, etc.
Traffic free zone - an area where vehicles have been prohibited.

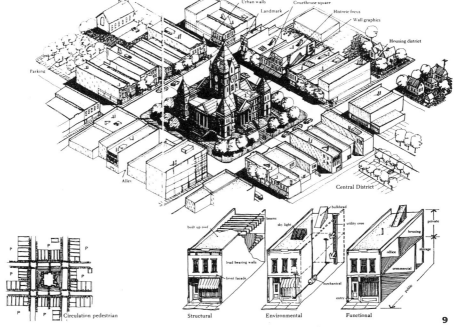

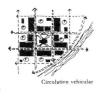

8

Circulation vehicular   Circulation pedestrian

Structural   Environmental   Functional   **9**

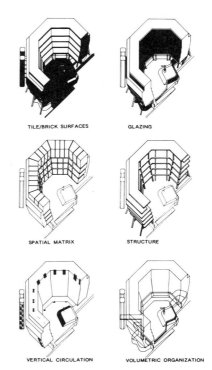

TILE/BRICK SURFACES   GLAZING

SPATIAL MATRIX   STRUCTURE

VERTICAL CIRCULATION   VOLUMETRIC ORGANIZATION

6 – 8 Report illustrations by Karl Bahr Deleon, J. Kargon, and Michael Plottel. Analysis of the Florey Building, Oxford, England, by James Stirling. From *Principles of Architectural Design,* James Tice (Ed.), Graduate School of Architecture, Planning, and Preservation, Columbia University, NY.

Slide Presentations

Commonly used for design presentations, slides have the distinct advantage of offering control over the sequence, scale, and focus of the images. Originally slides were used primarily to show existing work or to represent a designed environment through a series of photos of a realistic model; recently slide use has been extended to the presentation of drawings. These presentations provide another dimension, a sense of dynamics, to the presentation. The impact of a single drawing can be enhanced by creating diverse views through camera zooming or panning. Video editing and electronic color editing give slides expanded color representation.

6 – 9 Slide presentation by Steve Talley. Model photography. Garden Environments for Intergenerational Residents. Stanley Mendelsohn, Architect. Chris Harvey, Model builder.

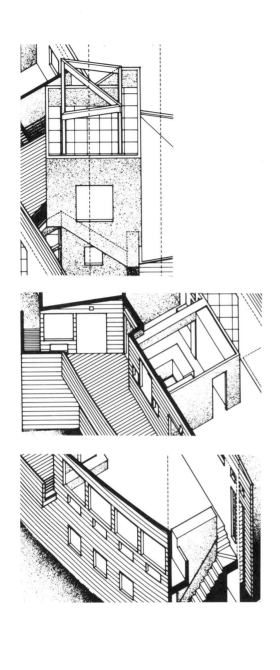

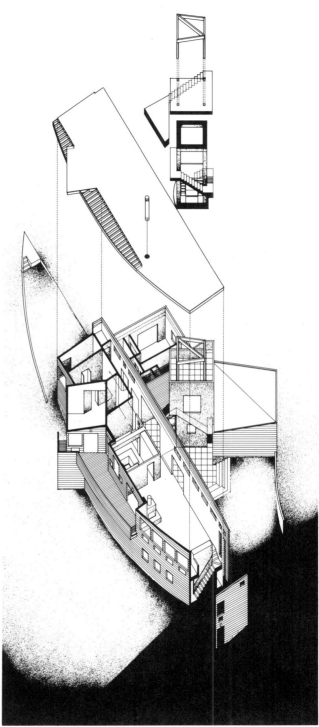

6 – 10 Exploded
axonometric rendering by
Mark English. Pen and ink on
mylar. Waldhauer Residence.
House + House,
Architects, San Francisco.

6 – 11 Hand-rendered perspective by Kevin Forseth. Computer graphic (Architrion) and pencil. House on Frederick Avenue, Milwaukee, WI.

Computer Graphics

As has been indicated several times in this book, computers have brought a revolutionary set of tools to drawing. As Marshall McLuhan pointed out, each new communication medium is initially used to mimic the content communicated by former media. Although, to date, computers have been used primarily to generate traditional drawings, designers are quickly beginning to understand the unique dimensions and possibilities of communicating with computers. Among the more significant differences between computer drawings and traditional drawings are: the immediacy of replication, a vast array of manipulation techniques, and the experience of graphic/visual media in motion. With computer graphics we may finally represent the dynamics of time, that fourth dimension the cubists sought. Computer graphics give us not only an alternative to drawing but also completely new tools for thinking. The impact on communication and design should be spectacular.

6 – 12 Base perspective construction by Kevin Forseth. Computer graphic (Architrion). House on Frederick Avenue, Milwaukee, WI.

6 – 13 Hand-rendered perspective by Kevin Forseth. Computer graphic (Architrion) and pencil. House on Frederick Avenue, Milwaukee, WI.

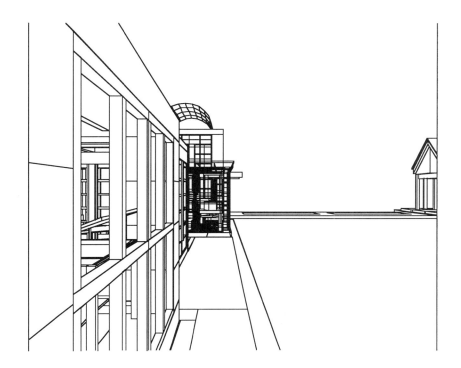

6 – 14 through 6 – 16
Perspectives by Kevin
Forseth. Computer graphic
(Architrion). House III.

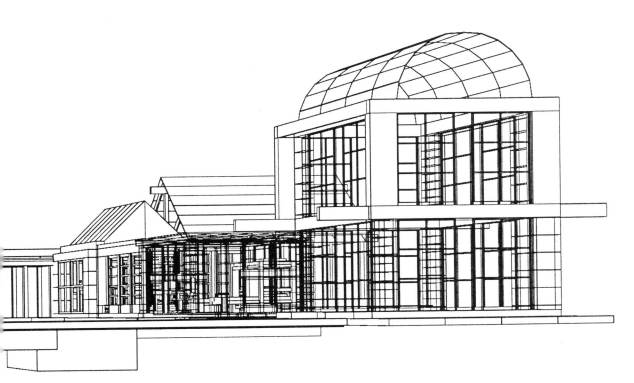

Video

Video technology has been used with drawings and other media to produce more dynamic presentations. With the introduction of new video graphic capabilities combined with the power of the computer, we can take advantage of an expanding set of new medium possibilities. Fully rendered color representation of space experienced in a kinesthetic manner is available. Editing capabilities in video allow access to a variety of image sources. The newly generated images improve not only the quality and scope of presentations, but also provide designers with new stimuli, which will affect the way they think about design. With the soon-to-be-adopted new standard for high-resolution video broadcasting, we should see video-compatible computer displays, making video available as a practical medium for depicting three-dimensional architectural space.

6 – 17 through 6 – 19
Video techniques. Video disk camera and computer renderings (Image Studio). First Baptist Church, Columbus, IN. Harry Weese, Architect.

120

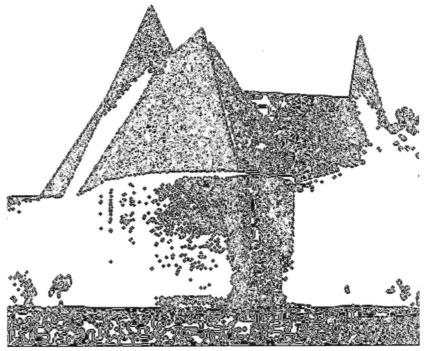

entry drive.

view to the commons.

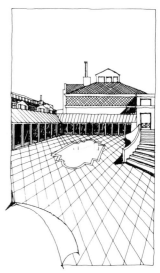

view of swimming/recreation area

6–20 Design study drawing by William L. Diefenbach, AIA. Pen. The Terraces, Los Gatos, CA. Stone Marraccini Patterson, Architects.

INSTRUMENTS

Anyone who has worked with both ink and pencil knows that they have different capabilities and characteristics, which affect drawings and the way designers think. Some designers have distinct preferences for a special type or manufacturer of a pen or pencil. Aware that different media can evoke different thoughts or perceptions, some designers are exploring a variety of media, including watercolor, oil paint, and sculpture as instruments for design exploration. Visual communication is not only affected by the special qualities or capabilities of these media but also by their limitations. Stubby pencils or paintbrushes, for example, may force one to focus on more general, abstract qualities of composition and avoid becoming absorbed in detail, while a fine-gauge technical pen might significantly slow the pace of freehand drawing, encouraging more deliberate and measured digestion of the images being generated.

6–21 Rendering by
Norman Kondy. Watercolor.
Design Guidelines and
Specific Plan for Highway
III, Indian Wells, CA.
Johnson, Fain and Pereira
Associates, Architects.

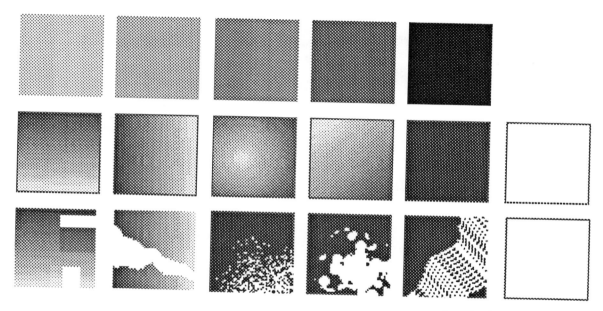

6 – 22 Demonstration of paint software. Computer graphic (Image Studio).

Electronic Instruments

Increasingly sophisticated computer graphics programs provide the designer with a wider array of drawing techniques and instruments, including pen and brush simulation. They can grab, pull, change, and alter in many ways line work or tone. There are two basic types of computer graphics instruments: "paint," or pixel based, and "draw," or object based. Paint programs work much like traditional graphics. Drawn images are "permanent" and can be changed by "painting" over the original drawing or by "cutting" away parts of the drawing. Currently paint programs provide the best capabilities for refinement in detail and color and the widest array of rendering instruments.

6 – 23 Rendered perspective, based on drawing by Kevin Forseth. Computer graphic (Architrion, Pixel Paint).

6 – 24 Rendered elevation using paint software. Computer graphic (Pixel Paint).

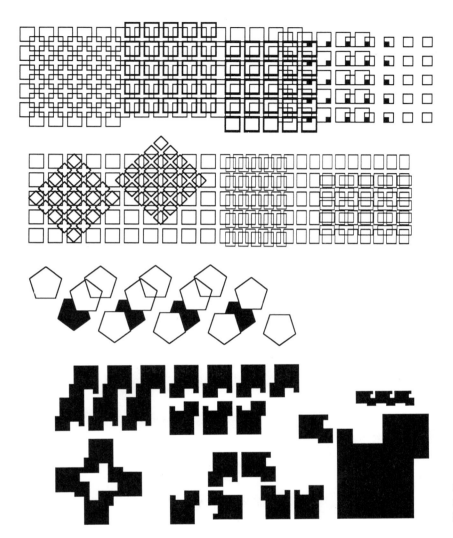

6 – 25 Demonstration of draw software. Computer graphic (Canvas).

Draw programs treat all elements of a drawing as independent objects, able to be transformed in shape, color, or scale at any time. Although draw programs lack the subtlety of paint programs, they can uniquely manipulate, extend, and alter images and are particularly suitable for design exploration. The "component" basis of draw programs also parallels the use of components in building construction. In emerging computer graphics programs, object-based drawings act as a visual representation of a data base, thus forming an active link between drawings and specifications. This may prove to be the most critical innovation of electronic drawing.

6 – 26 Fenestration study using draw software. Computer graphic (Canvas).

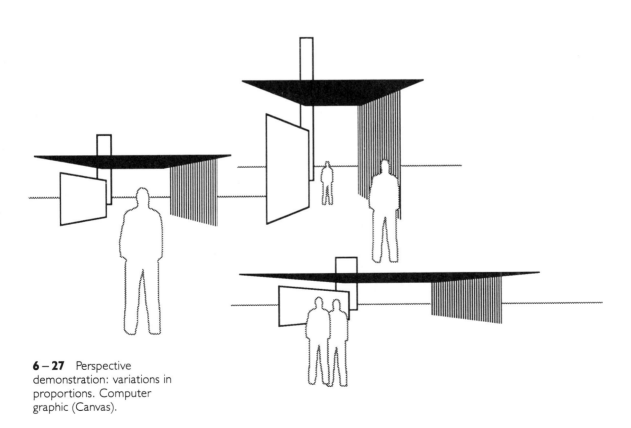

6 – 27 Perspective demonstration: variations in proportions. Computer graphic (Canvas).

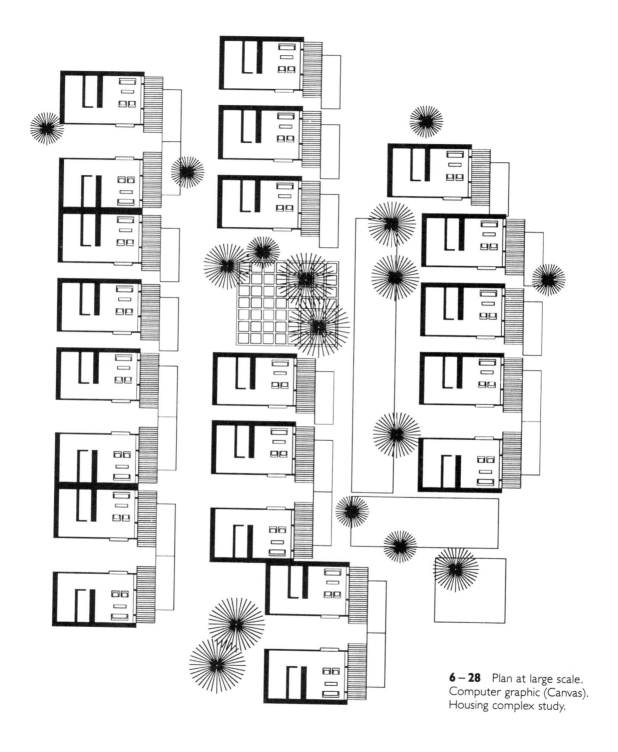

6 – 28 Plan at large scale. Computer graphic (Canvas). Housing complex study.

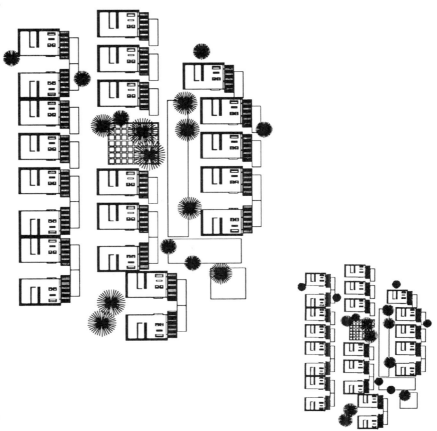

6 – 29 Plan at medium scale. Computer graphic (Canvas). Housing complex study.

6 – 30 Plan at small scale. Computer graphic (Canvas). Housing complex study.

FEATURES

Visual communication can be significantly affected by our approach to the use of media. If we understand the range of variables at our command for conveying images and how that affects communication, we can gain control over other dimensions of drawing, opening up additional options.

Size

One of the distinct advantages of visual communication is its ability to send simultaneous messages. We can read a visual image at several different levels: as an overall graphic composition in space; as pattern; as color and light; and as detail and texture. The size of a drawing can often affect the number and levels of communication that can be derived from that drawing. A large-scale rendition of a drawing invites one to look at it in more depth and peruse its various parts. A smaller reproduction of the same drawing keeps our focus on the overall abstract level.

Alignment Analysis

Alignment Alternative

Various types of route alignment systems were studied in context with the Indianapolis Urban environment, the 'loop', the 'line', and the 'cross'; and many alignment courses were also analyzed. After a comprehensive study which studied the major public facilities, activity zones, pedestrian generators, historic monuments, land uses, visitor destinations, employment centers, future development opportunities and many other urban factors; a preliminary route and station locations were developed.

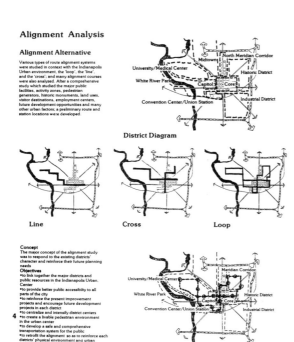

District Diagram

Line   Cross   Loop

Concept
The major concept of the alignment study was to respond to the existing districts' character and reinforce their future planning needs

Objectives
•to link together the major districts and public resources in the Indianapolis Urban Center
•to provide better public accessibility to all parts of the city
•to reinforce the present improvement projects and encourage future development projects in each district
•to centralize and intensify district centers
•to create a livable pedestrian environment in the urban center
•to develop a safe and comprehensive transportation system for the public
•to retrofit the alignment so as to reinforce each districts' physical environment and urban design objectives
•to interface present activity zones and create new ones

Alignment Diagram

Planning Considerations

This chart is to show briefly the characteristics of the districts studied and some of their objectives and urban design considerations. Some of the urban design considerations are being studied individually, but it is the purpose of this study to unify and intensify these development projects and link them to each other by the automated system.

Districts	Character	Urban Design Objectives
University/Medical Center District	•a growing urban university •a major sport complex •the largest state medical research facility	•to link the University and the Medical Center to the Downtown Center •to develop the transition area around the district •to create a cohesiveness to the district
Midtown District	•a residential neighborhood with a declining commercial and industrial node •a historic canal corridor •a major medical complex	•to redevelop and revitalize the residential and commercial fabric •to redevelop the canal corridor and parkway •to link the district to the city's public resources
North Meridian Corridor	•a major urban entry to the core •a significant historical open space and park •a linear urban wall and edge development	•to intensify the linear urban wall development •to create an urban gateway to the core •to decrease the vehicular congestion
Historic District	•location of several historical residential districts •a significant historical commercial area •location of new housing developments	•to tie and unify the historical districts •to develop support facilities for the district •to provide a public transportation system for the new developments and link the area with the public resources of the city
Downtown Core	•an intensely developed urban area •an office, financial and retail center •a public activity magnet •a historic monument	•to continue developing a safe pedestrian circulation system •to link the core with other major pedestrian generators •to intensify future development
Industrial District	•a predominant industrial and commercial land use •served by interstates, rail, and arterial streets •a major industrial headquarters center	•to develop and intensify the (in city) industrial district •to link the industrial district to the pedestrian activities and resources
Convention Center/Union Station District	•a major C.B.D. activity generator •a significant historical rail station, proposed to be a ground transportation center •a major stadium in the planning stage	•to link this activity center to the other pedestrian generators •to intensify development and add support facilities •to further develop the transportation node with the automated system
State Capitol Complex	•a historic landmark •a major state government office complex •an important physical and activity node	•to develop a strong public link to the downtown core •to develop public accessibility from the complex to the other city districts
White River Corridor	•a linear waterway system, park and recreation network	•to develop the corridor into a public scenic waterway and parkway system •to create an active urban park •to link and develop public access from the park to the urban core

4   5

6 – 31 through 6 – 33
Report presentations by Harry Eggink. Offset printing. Automated Transit System, Urban Design Study, Indianapolis, IN.

Format

Another way to manipulate, and therefore control, the communication of images is through the use of format. Format establishes a context or framework within which we can understand various parts of a presentation. In a single drawing, format composition provides a means of emphasizing some drawings as primary and relegating other drawings to support roles. This same formatting ability in a multiple-image, sequential presentation such as a report is important because we must retain a mental image of the framework or hierarchy as we proceed through the sequence. The format continuously reinforces an order, starting with major divisions of the report and then moving down within those divisions to reveal more detail.

Market Square Station Alternatives

Station Alternative A

Site
The station is to be incorporated into the elevated pedestrian overpass that spans over Alabama St. connecting the Arena to the City Market

Urban Design Opportunities
• to link the Arena directly (enclosed) to the City Market
• to reinforce the 2nd level pedestrian system so that it would tie the Government Center, City Market, Arena, Parking, and Offices together
• to encourage new development north of the Market
• to intensify the activities of Market Square

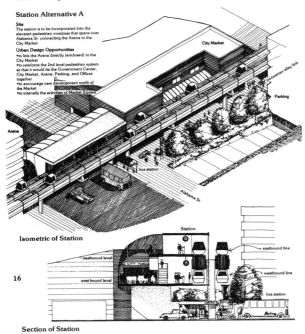

Isometric of Station

16

Section of Station

Station Alternative B

Site
The station is to be located behind the old city market in the pedestrian alley, and to be incorporated into the old city market

Urban Design Opportunities
• to link the station directly to the highly active pedestrian generator, the City Market
• to reinforce the 2nd level pedestrian system so that it would tie the Government Center, City Market, Parking, Arena, and Offices together
• to intensify the activities of Market Square
• to reinforce the public accessibility to Market Square

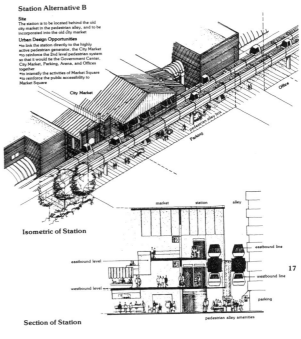

Isometric of Station

17

Section of Station

Automated System Opportunities

Neighborhood Transit Center

Objectives
• to provide a public center for the neighborhood
• to develop a neighborhood transportation node
• to create a livable public 'place'
• to provide accessibility for the residents to the city resources

Athenaeum District

Objectives
• to develop a community center and focus for the elderly and its neighbors
• to provide a passive recreational zone for the residents
• to create a vital and active urban space

Washington Transit Mall

Objectives
• to tie in with the Washington Steet Transit Mall
• to link with the bus network
• to link with the pedestrian circulation system

18

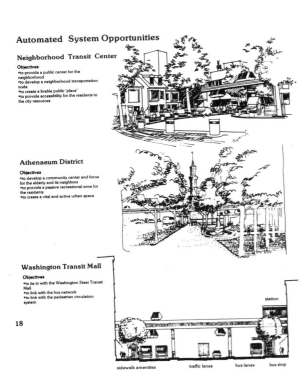

Office Complex Station

Objectives
• to be incorporated into an active public indoor space
• to link directly with the vertical transportation system of the complex
• to reinforce the enclosed public second level circulation system

Urban Park

Objectives
• to intensify the public awareness and use of these small urban parks
• to encourage future urban park development
• to link these parks to the public transportation system

Intercept Parking

Objectives
• to reinforce parking systems in relationship with the interstate and outside the city core
• to provide a direct link to the city core
• to integrate the automated system with the city bus network

19

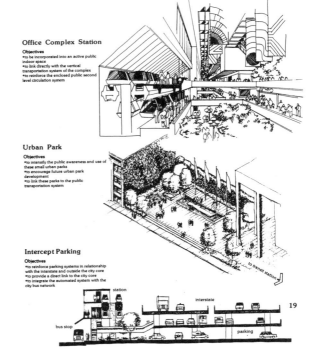

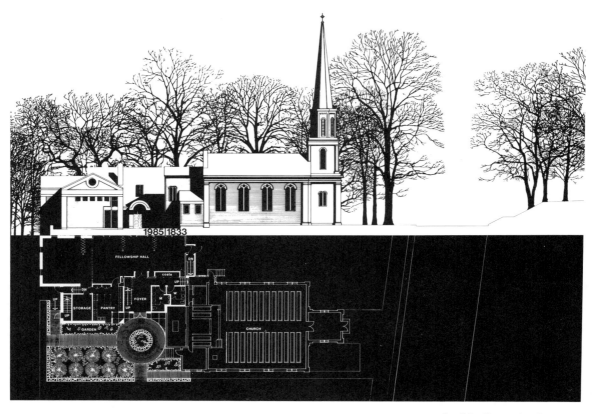

6 – 34 Illustration by Richard Bergmann, FAIA. Pen and ink. St. Michael's Lutheran Church and Parish Hall. Richard Bergmann, Architects.

Definition

The level of detail one includes in a drawing can also affect visual communication. The inclusion of selective detail can determine where we look in the drawing and the sequence or structure of ideas that are communicated. The designer may also purposely distort frameworks or formats in order to give special emphasis or to shift perceptions about known objects. A designer may choose to create an in-focus foreground by presenting an out-of-focus background. Or enlargements of detail can be superimposed on overview drawings.

6 – 35 Distorted format in a presentation, based on a drawing by Jim Stutzman. Computer graphic (Architrion). MuseHouse. Stutzman & Associates, Architects.

133

6 – 36 Illustration by Richard Conway Meyer. Pantone marker. Adaptive reuse of Eastern State Penitentiary. Richard Conway Meyer, Architect.

STYLE

Another kind of drawing option is embodied in the secondary messages that one communicates through the style of drawing. Style options can be powerful tools in the hands of a designer because they can convey hidden messages, as opposed to the more obvious messages provided by the content or subject. Just as a style of speaking—a particular voice intonation, for example—has long been recognized as extremely important to effective oral communication, style in drawing adds a level of refinement that distinguishes the very effective visual communicator from the adequate communicator.

6 – 37 Illustration by Wilbur Pearson. Pencil on vellum. Tequesta Cove. John J. Sklanka, Architect.

6 – 38 Sketch by Antoine Predock. Pastel and ink. Fine Arts Complex, Arizona State University. Antoine Predock, FAIA, Architect.

6 – 39 Illustration by Craig Roberts, Designer, Ft. Lauderdale, FL. Marker on rice paper.

Identity

The influx of computer-generated drawings in the field of architecture and design has been accompanied by a heightened appreciation for the hand-drawn sketch. Traditional sketches convey the presence of a human being at the other end of a communication, which many clients find comforting. Styles of drawing may eventually emerge in the electronic media, but for the present they are marked by the lack of a personal stamp. Most contemporary designers have evolved a style of drawing that fits with their own personality and their own interests. A consistent use of this style gives the drawing an identity and association with a particular designer.

6 – 40 Sketch by Michael E. Doyle. Marker and color pencil on pastel paper. Venazza, Italy.

6 – 41 Sketch study as a source for ideas by Jerry Exline. Felt pen.

6 – 42 Stylized presentation drawings by Dick Sneary. Felt pen on marker paper. Bufman Amphitheater, Phoenix, AZ. Hellmuth Obata Kassabaum, Architects.

Attitude

Through their style, drawings can also convey certain information about the attitudes of the designer toward his subject, his audience, and the purposes of communication. When working with a residential client, architects will often have a draftsman construct a perspective using precise geometric techniques. They then overlay the constructed perspective with yellow tracing paper, on which a freehand version of the drawing is produced. The freehand style of the drawing suggests to the client that the purpose of the drawing is to encourage relaxed, informal conversation and not to convey a fixed, unassailable design. Through the drawing the architect is inviting the client to engage in a dialogue about the design. With style, drawings can also convey the designer's sense of discipline, energy, vitality, or enthusiasm. These can be especially reassuring to clients having their first experience working with an architect, since they are proceeding on the basis of their trust in the architect.

6 – 43 Stylized presentation drawing by Dick Dee. Ink. Barnett Plaza, Edward D. Stone and Associates PA, Planners and Landscape Architects. Harwood Taylor/HKS, Architects.

6 – 44 Sketch illustration by Dick Sneary. Felt pen. Bufman Amphitheater, Phoenix, AZ. Hellmuth Obata Kassabaum, Architects.

6 – 45 Rendering by Michael Sechman. Pencil on vellum. First and Mission, Houston, TX. Skidmore, Owings and Merrill-Houston, Architects.

Mood

Even with the aid of computer graphics, it is not possible for the designer to convey all of the intended qualities of the piece of architecture. In some cases the designer may not even know about specific detailed decisions at the early stages of design; to attempt to be more precise might be misleading. What designers often communicate to their clients is the direction in which they intend to take the design and the qualities of environment they would like to create. Through the style of the drawing, a designer can convey the exuberance, the serenity, the solemnity, or the informality of the evolving design.

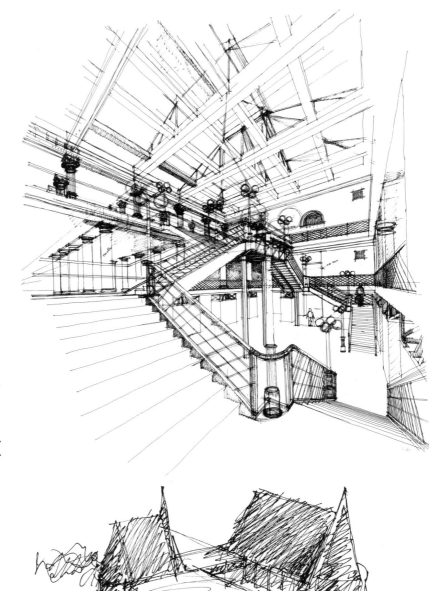

6–46 Dynamic illustration by Dick Sneary. Ink on vellum, freehand over computer layout. St. Louis Post Office Competition, St. Louis, MO. PBNI Architects.

6–47 Informal sketch. Felt pen. First Baptist Church, Columbus, IN. Harry Weese, Architect.

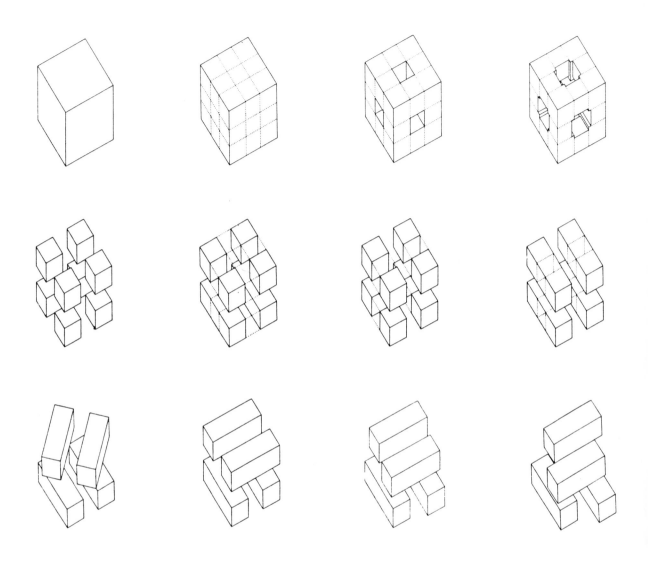

7 – 1 Axonometric views by Peter Eisenman. Ink. House IV, from *Peter Eisenman Houses of Cards* by Peter Eisenman.

ABSTRACTION

7

Drawings are stand-ins for the real environment they represent. They are not duplicates of that environment; they are representations. All drawings are more abstract than the concrete reality of the actual environment. Among the drawing options available to a designer is the adjustment or selection of the level of abstraction at which a subject is represented. At the most abstract level, drawings become a set of symbols that stand in for larger or more complex subjects. The use of symbols allows one to be very economical in manipulating representations of large amounts of information. Given the complexity of most architectural design, this type of diagrammatic language is extremely useful in expediting thinking. While abstract drawings can be extremely useful tools, it is important to keep in mind that they are only as effective and useful as the viewer's knowledge of what they represent. And so, where they might be very helpful in communication among peers, fellow members of the design team, they may be misleading when used as means of communication between designer and client.

Abstraction not only allows for alternate representations of physical environments such as buildings, spaces, and their components, but it also provides the opportunity to represent the very important nonphysical realities of environmental experience, such as paths of circulation, angles of views, space zoning, hierarchy of use, and intensity of activity. At another level removed from the actual content of design, abstract drawings can provide a graphic representation of programmatic and conceptual concerns, providing the designer with information in a more usable form. This chapter will explore a range of abstract representations, from that of the concrete physical reality to the most abstract type of drawing, discussing abstraction as editing, model, and diagram.

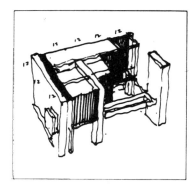
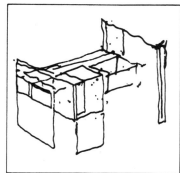
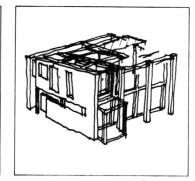
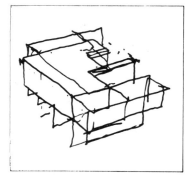

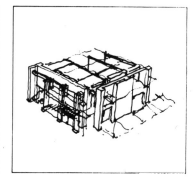
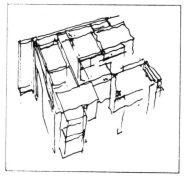
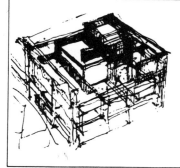

ABSTRACTION AS EDITING

In the process of design, we often must focus attention on specific aspects of the environment, such as structure, enclosure, or circulation. One device for focusing emphasizes an element by rendering all the other elements in a more diagrammatic manner. The realistic aspects of the significant elements are thus emphasized while the overall context is retained as a background. Another approach is to extract the items to be emphasized from their normal context and render them in a simplified manner that indicates relationships without involving the concrete details of their construction.

7 – 2 Design sketches by Peter Eisenman. Pen. From *Peter Eisenman Houses of Cards* by Peter Eisenman.

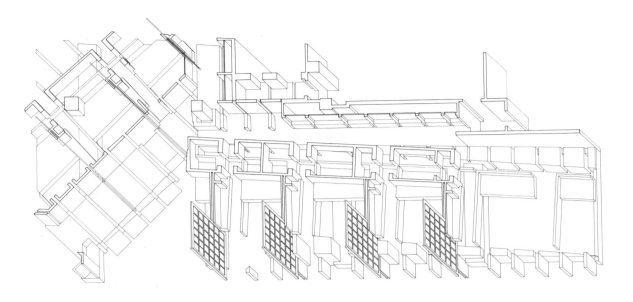

7 – 3 Axonometric view by Peter Eisenman. Ink. Tom's Loft, New York, NY. Eisenman and Yorgancioglu, Architects.

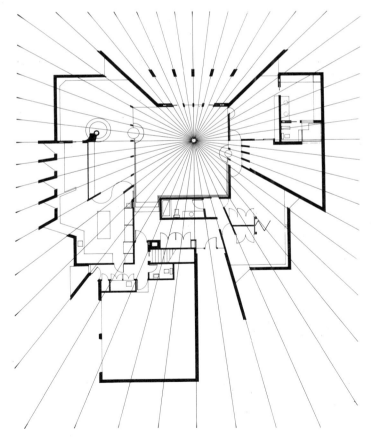

7 – 4 Plan study by Gunnar Birkerts. Ink. Freeman Residence. Gunnar Birkerts & Associates Inc., Architects.

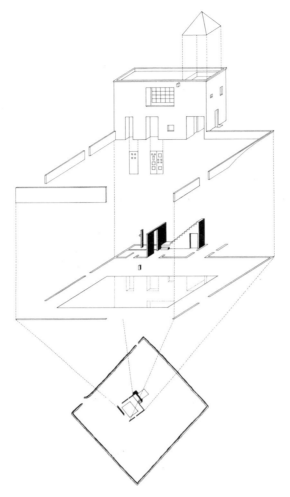

ABSTRACT MODELS

The architectural designer's constant concern is the integration of many components into a synthesized whole so that all of the components of design work together to achieve a common purpose. The number and complexity of components that an environment or building comprises requires the designer to develop abstract views of the overall environment, providing a representation of the general properties of the components and their relationships. While designers could construct physical models for these purposes, it is generally sufficient and more practical to sketch views of such models. In three-dimensional computer graphics, we can construct abstract models and obtain as many views as we could with a physical model; we can also generate transparent or interior views not possible with a physical model.

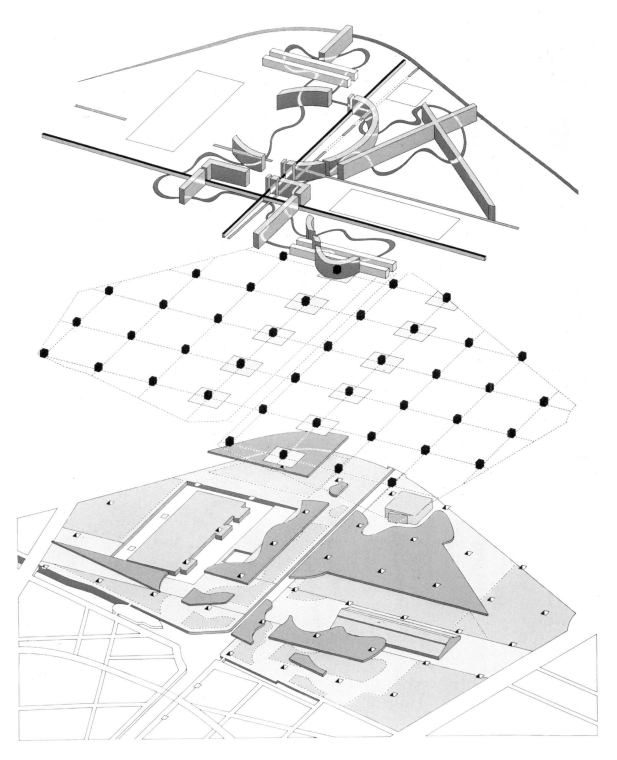

147

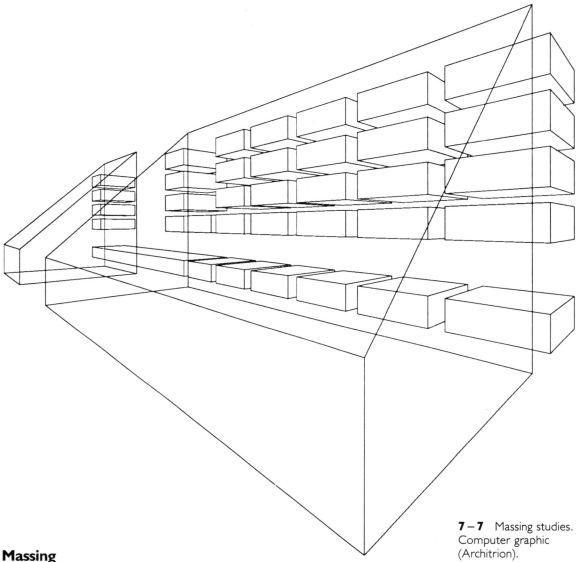

Massing

The three-dimensional zoning, orientation, and configuration of
space in an environment can often be manipulated and studied
more easily through the use of drawings that show the basic massing
of space. These quick sketches can provide a rapid means of com-
paring several alternatives. The introduction of three-dimensional
computer graphics promises to assist greatly in the modeling of
massing because manipulation and replication are easy, point of view
can be rapidly changed, and quantitative accounts of such things as
square footage or volume of the spaces being modeled are simple
to maintain.

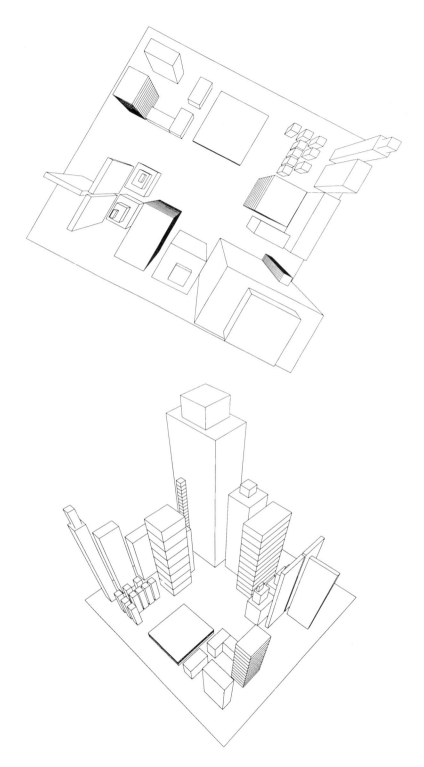

7 – 8 and 7 – 9 Massing studies by Paul Lew. Computer graphic (Architrion).

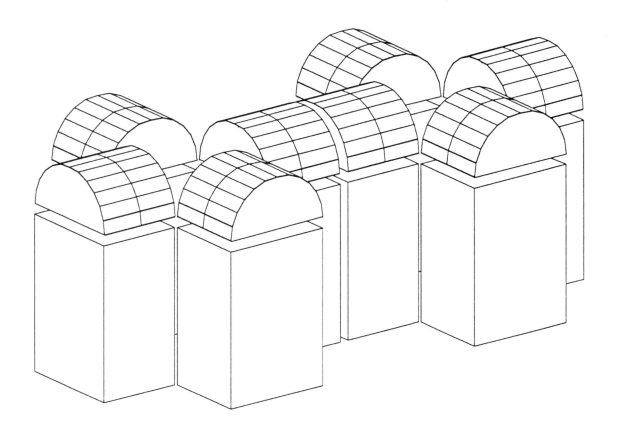

Negative Space

Architects often talk about space as the essence of architecture, and yet they do not often try to represent space as an element for study. Analysis of the three-dimensional negative space within a building can provide important views that will enhance the development of spatial unity and thereby the overall unity of the architecture. Focusing on space rather than structure can provide fresh insights into the nature of the design problem and initiate new avenues of thought. We might think of space as a fluid, structure, or barrier.

7 – 10 through 7 – 12
Negative space studies.

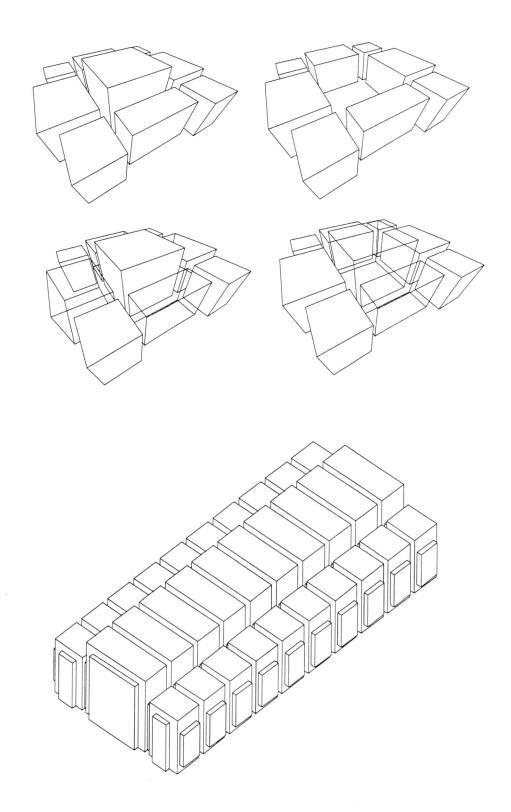

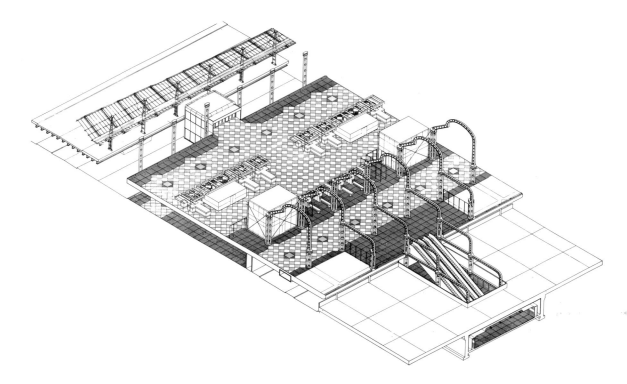

7 – 13 Skeleton paraline projection by Murphy/Jahn. Ink. United Airlines Terminal I Complex, O'Hare International Airport, Chicago, IL. Murphy/Jahn, Architects.

Skeleton

A counterpart of the model of negative space is the modeling of frameworks or skeletons of selected systems that permeate an entire building, such as structure, circulation paths, HVAC, or communication systems. This again is an area in which three-dimensional computer graphics will be a great help, allowing the designer to develop the various systems in conjunction with each other but, at any given time, to see them as separate systems in three-dimensional space.

7 – 14 Skeleton perspective by Steven Holl. Ink. American Memorial Library, Berlin. Steven Holl Architects.

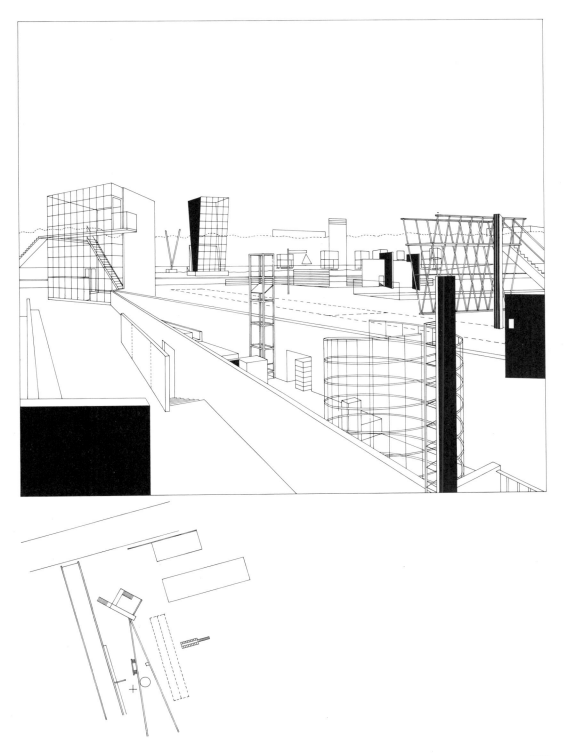

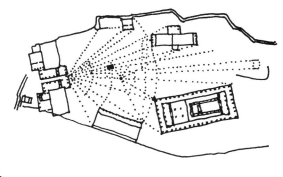

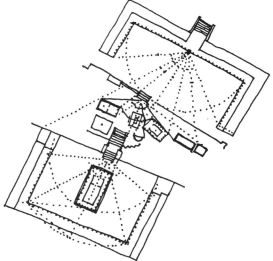

7 – 15 Plan diagrams by Paul Lew. Felt pen. Athens Acropolis and Pergamon, after drawings by Doxiadis.

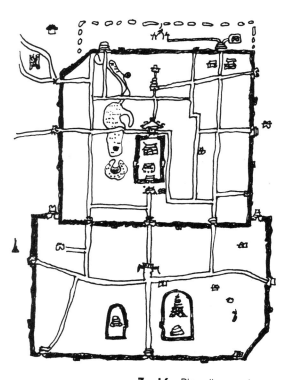

7 – 16 Plan diagram by Paul Lew. Felt pen. Beijing.

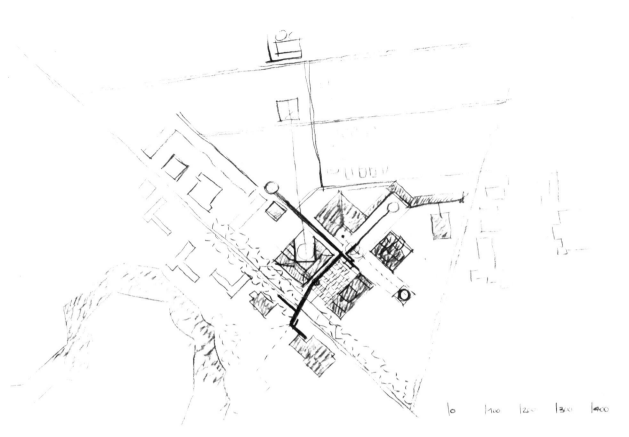

7 – 17 Plan diagram by
Romaldo Giurgola. Pencil.
Student Union/Library, New
York State University
College, Plattsburgh.
Mitchell/Giurgola,
Architects.

ABSTRACT DIAGRAMS

To deal with the complexities and intangibles of various systems,
professionals in many different fields have developed their own
abstract language to represent the things that they study; mathe-
matics, chemistry, physics, music, and dance each have their own
systems of notation. Several fields, including architecture, use a diagrammatic language through which identities, objects, and their relationships can be symbolized. As with all languages, symbol usage
and meaning must be consistent if they are to be economical and
effective. Consistency can be achieved through the selection of symbols or the underlying ordering convention.

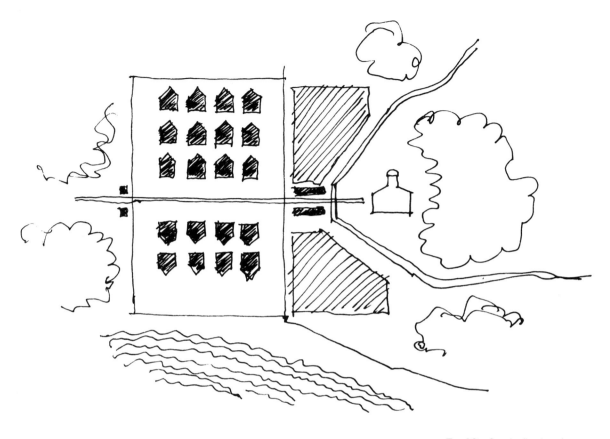

7 – 18 Symbolic drawings. Felt pen.

Symbols

A key element in any diagrammatic language is the set of symbols used to represent specific identities or objects. Because these symbols stand in for objects, they must be recognizable and distinct from one another. This might be done by the use of a profile, such as a house or a church, the use of signs, such as the Greek cross for medical buildings, the Latin cross for churches, the Star of David for synagogues, and a book for libraries. Symbols might also be initials, such as LR for living room, K for kitchen, B for bath.

To facilitate the rapid reading that diagrams intend, the symbols must be distinguishable from one another but also readable as a family of items. As in verbal language or the typewritten alphabet, a balance has to be sought between consistencies of the set and distinction of the individual elements.

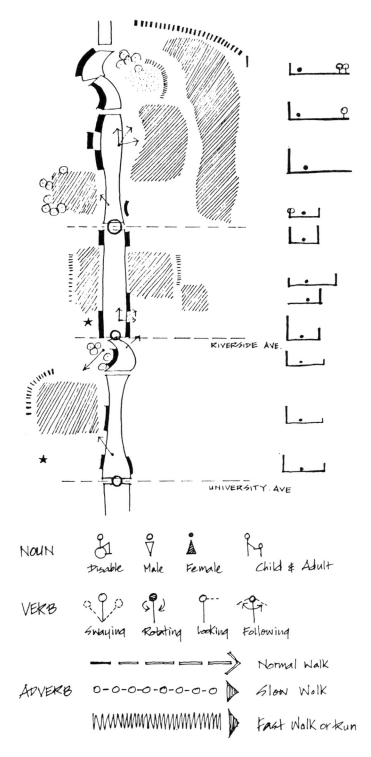

RIVERSIDE AVE.

UNIVERSITY. AVE

NOUN — Disable, Male, Female, Child & Adult

VERB — Swaying, Rotating, Looking, Following

ADVERB — Normal Walk, Slow Walk, Fast Walk or Run

7 – 19 and 7 – 20
Symbolic drawings by
Hao-wei Yu. Felt pen. From
*The Role of Integrated
Representation of
Architectural Space and
Human Behavior*, Masters
Thesis in Architecture.

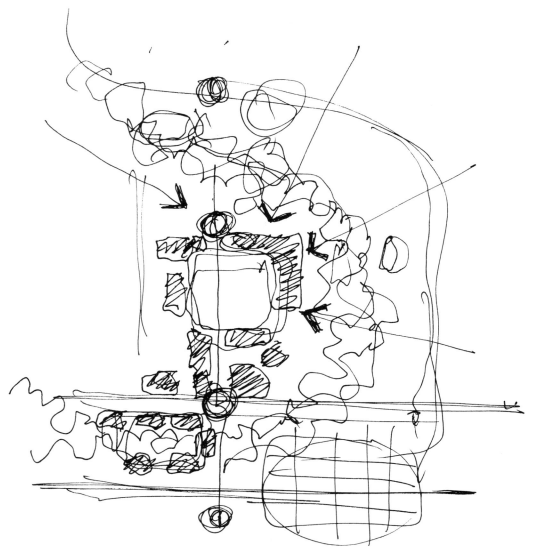

Relationships

Designers are fundamentally concerned with relationships among entities and therefore use diagrams to represent these relationships in an abstract shorthand. Relationships can be indicated by proximity, orientation, or the introduction of linear elements that show some specific connections between entities. The utility of diagrams is increased by the ability to introduce qualifiers to both identities and the relationships being represented. These qualifiers can symbolize the nature of the relationships or the identities, the scale or hierarchy of elements, and the intensity of relationships.

7 – 21 Relationship drawing, based on plan drawing. Felt pen.

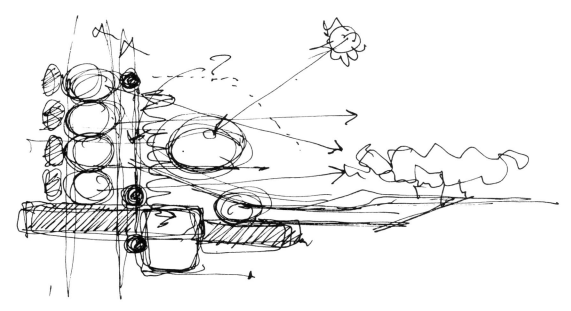

7 – 22 Relationship drawing, based on section drawing. Felt pen.

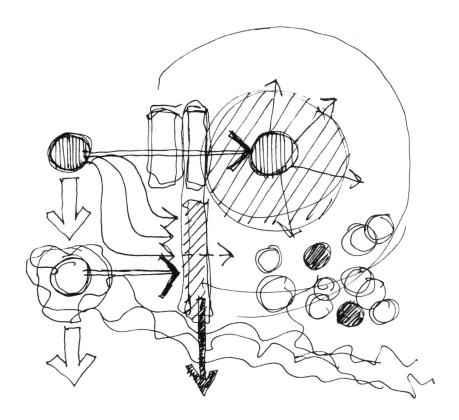

7 – 23 Relationship drawing, non spatial. Felt pen.

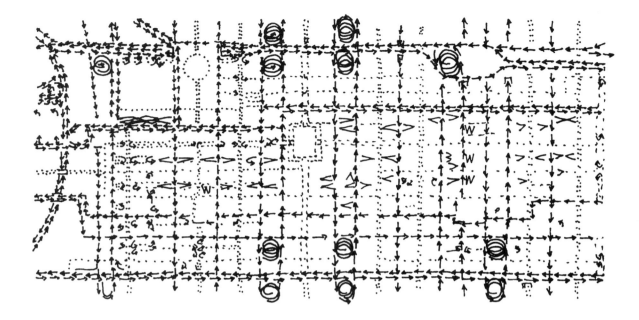

7 – 24 Sketch diagram, based on drawing by Louis I. Kahn, by Paul Lew. Felt pen. Philadelphia City Plan 1952 – 53.

DYNAMICS

A key attribute of abstraction is the ability to transcend the normal boundaries of physical modeling to illustrate dynamic relationships among entities or elements. Whether using abstraction as editing, modeling, or diagraming, the designer can illustrate changes over time, movement, transitions, and transformations as well as the overall nature of several different kinds of processes.

Movement

Environments are not just compositions of static elements. They change in a number of ways—in use, in density of activity, through reactions to climate, or through adaptation for special occasions. Abstractions can help clarify the dynamics of such things as the movement of the sun, whether across the face of a building or as a pattern of light moving within a room. Computer graphics will pro-vide some other new tools to animate the representation of such movement, more realistically modeling and highlighting attributes such as sequence, schedule, or pattern in the environment.

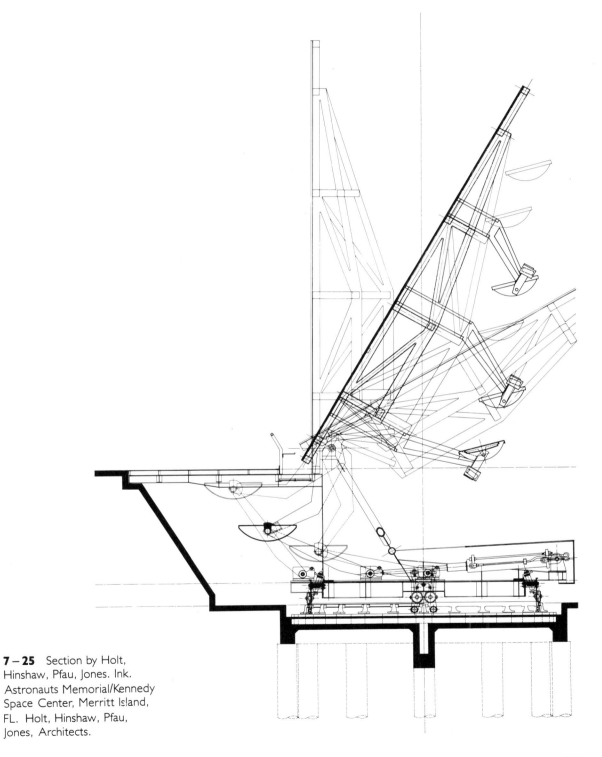

7–25 Section by Holt, Hinshaw, Pfau, Jones. Ink. Astronauts Memorial/Kennedy Space Center, Merritt Island, FL. Holt, Hinshaw, Pfau, Jones, Architects.

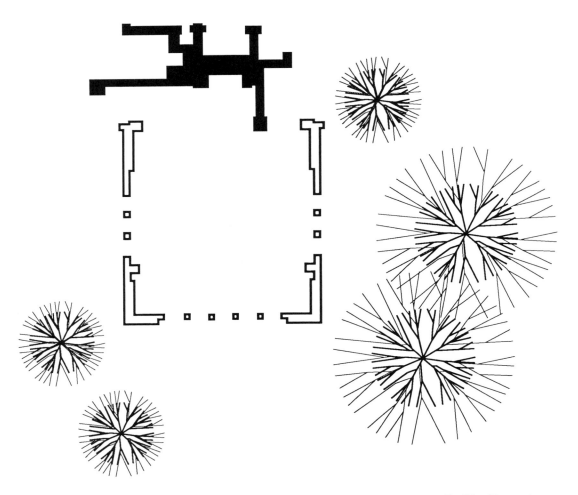

7 – 26 Change in context over time. Computer graphic (Canvas).

Change

Designed environments and their settings may intentionally or unintentionally undergo change over time. Modeling these changes, which directly affect design decisions, helps us to understand their nature as well as their effects. Such things as the pace or acceleration of change can have great impact on an environment.

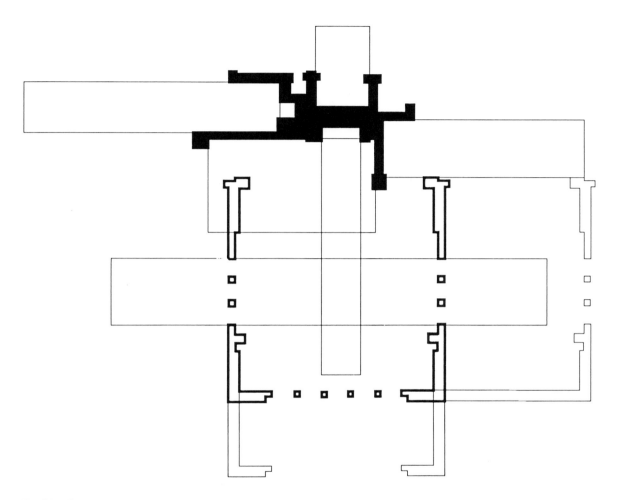

7 – 27 Change as transformation. Computer graphic (Canvas).

Transformation

Often environments or buildings are designed to be responsive to exterior change by undergoing transformations themselves. These transformations may take place over the span of an hour, a day, or several years. They might vary seasonally, yearly, or over longer periods. Modeling such transformations helps the designer explain their importance to the client.

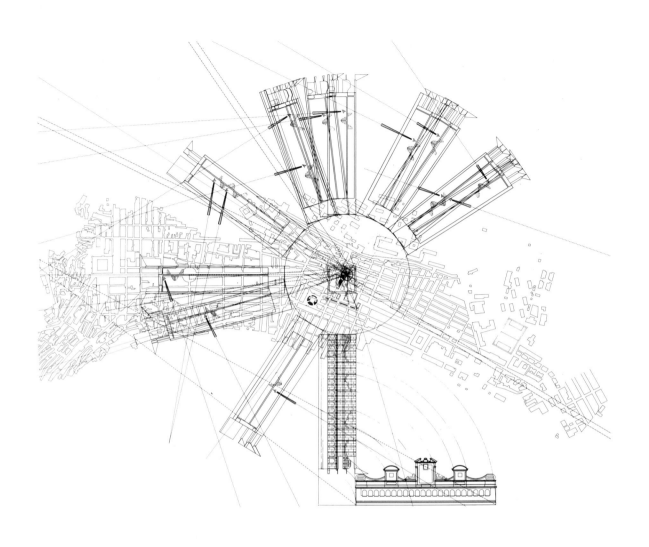

8 – 1   The Construction of
the Tower by Jorge Silvetti.
Ink. Four Public Squares,
Leonforte, Sicily, 1983. Jorge
Silvetti, Designer.

EXPLORATIONS

8

Irrespective of media or technique, drawing should be considered a constantly evolving process rather than a fixed set of methods. The design process is reinforced by a vitality in drawing that is derived from constant exploration and experimentation.

Since drawings were used as a means to design, architects and designers have constantly modified various drawing techniques and invented new approaches, combinations of techniques, and conventions to meet different communication needs. A review of some of these explorations provides options for direct use now, as well as ways of thinking about drawing options that may promote the invention of additional drawing options.

Various articles and books by researchers such as Robert Greenstreet, Kevin Forseth, and Douglas Cooper illustrate that considerable experimentation followed the invention of perspective and other conventions. But over time we have tended to standardize the way we think of these conventions. The examples in this chapter will review some of the more original and recent drawing variations and the different approaches one might take toward drawing conventions. Particular emphasis is given to the use of color, which is emerging as a practical new dimension to design drawing as sophisticated computer graphic and color reproduction technologies become more accessible for on-line design work.

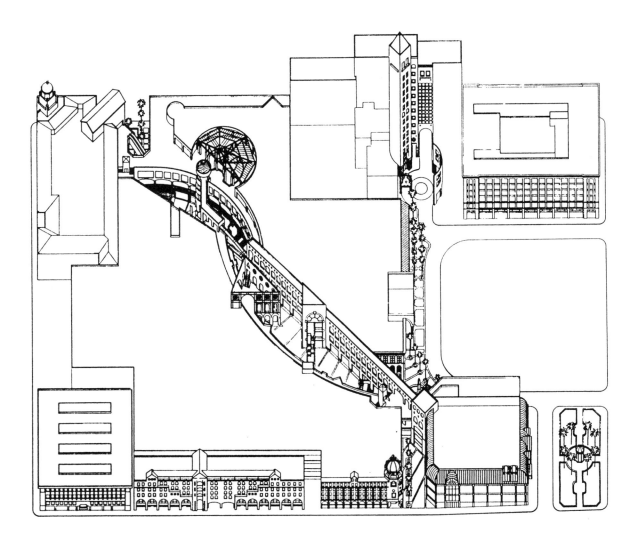

Designers use combinations of a variety of conventions, such as plan or section perspective, and orthographic or paraline projection. These allow them to free up their view of a project from the constraints of any one specific convention and bring the different drawing approaches into close proximity, giving them an opportunity to shift perceptions and to take fresh views of the project.

8 – 2 Plan projection by The Jerde Partnership. Ink. The Horton Plaza, San Diego, CA. The Jerde Partnership, Architects.

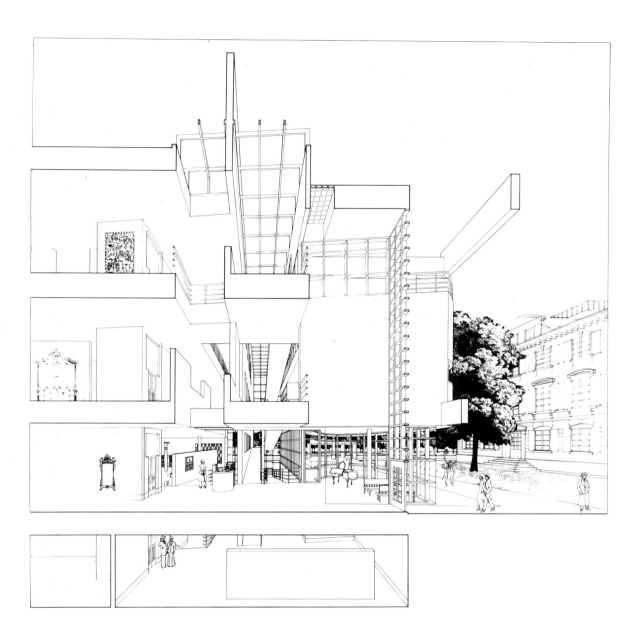

8 – 3 Section perspective
by Richard Meier &
Partners. Ink. Museum for
the Decorative Arts,
Frankfurt. Richard Meier &
Partners, Architects.

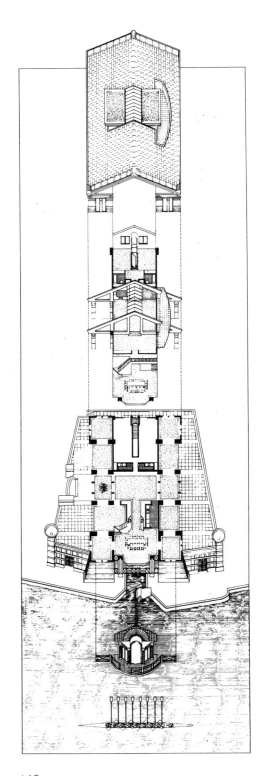

8 – 4 Disassembled plan projection by Terry Farrell. Ink. Henley on Thames Royal Regatta Headquarters, London. Terry Farrell & Company, Ltd.

COLOR

The tradition of colored architectural rendering dates from at least its prominent use at the Ecole des Beaux-Arts in Paris in the nineteenth century. By the turn of the century, teachers and students at the school were demonstrating the power and subtlety of color in depicting the breadth of sensations of architectural space in light. The colored rendering survives to this day as the primary means for the realistic depiction of architecture. Until recently, contemporary practice relegated the colored rendering to client promotional material because of the time and expense required to create it. If color was used at all for design study drawings, it was used in a more simplistic or abstract manner, in the faster media of pencil or markers. Many architects do not use colored sketches as the primary means of evaluating design decisions but rely on a combination of material and color samples and their memory or imagination.

8 – 5 Rendering by Hoffpauir/Rosner Studio. Watercolor. Lobby interior for Harvard Medical School, Building C. Tsoi Kobus & Associates, Architects.

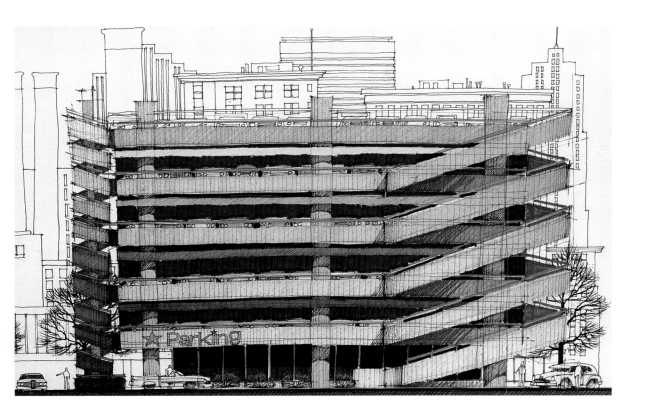

8–6 Perspective rendering by Howard Associates, Sylvania, OH. Ink and watercolor. Orlando Galleria Design Study, Orlando, FL. RTKL Associates, Inc., Architects.

8–7 Rendering by Christopher Grubbs. Prismacolor on paper. Hyatt Fantasy Resort, Mexico, 1987. Gail S. Grant, Architect.

8–8 Rendering by Michael E. Doyle. Prismacolor and marker on Strathmore bristol board. Color studies for a parking garage.

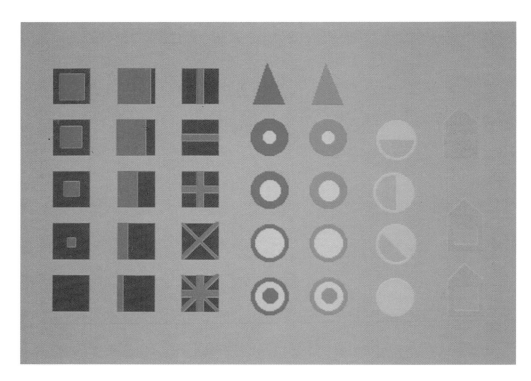

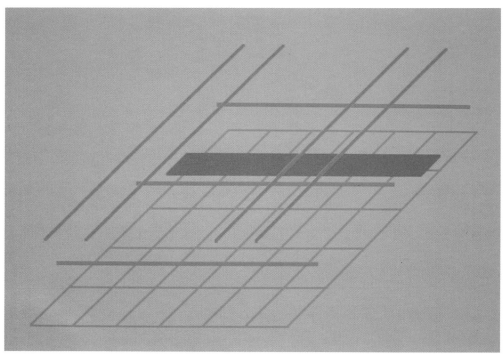

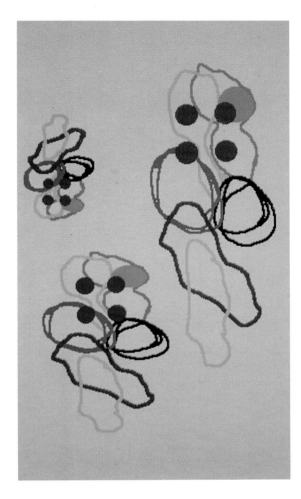

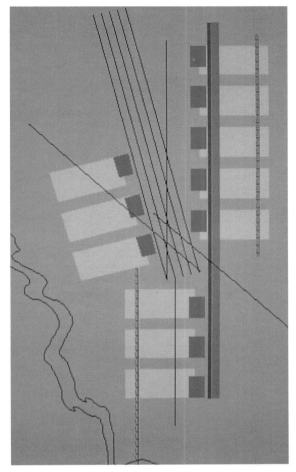

8 – 9 Color symbol sets. Computer graphic (Canvas).

8 – 10 Grid manipulations. Computer graphic (Canvas).

8 – 11 Explorations of spatial relationships. Computer graphic (Canvas).

8 – 12 Studies of spatial rhythms. Computer graphic (Canvas).

Symbolic Color

Our ability to recognize even slight differences in color makes it very useful for diagrams of complex relationships during the problem analysis and schematic design phases of a project. Colored diagrams are used often in conceptual drawings to help organize information and depict subtle variations. With the advent of computer graphics, symbolic color has taken on an even more powerful role, depicting the relationships of building systems in three-dimensional space. Colors for computer drawings were originally limited to a few basic hues, but today designers have a full range of color available and can adjust color hue, intensity, and value more precisely with computers than with traditional media. The ease with which color can be manipulated on computers should have a considerable effect on architects' use of and sensitivity to color.

173

Computer-aided Color Renderings

The introduction of three-dimensional modeling, color, and light modeling to computer graphics is making color rendering available to architects as a means to study and create designs. The availability of reliable, realistic tools for environmental simulation changes the questions of design from what is possible to what is appropriate. Tomorrow's designer will of necessity be more knowledgeable about color theory and the interactions of light and space. One can hope that this will have a very positive effect on the quality of architectural design.

8 – 13 through 8 – 15
Rendered perspectives by Antoine Fatio. Computer graphic (Architrion II and Studio 8). Beach House. Clement Difillippo, Architect.

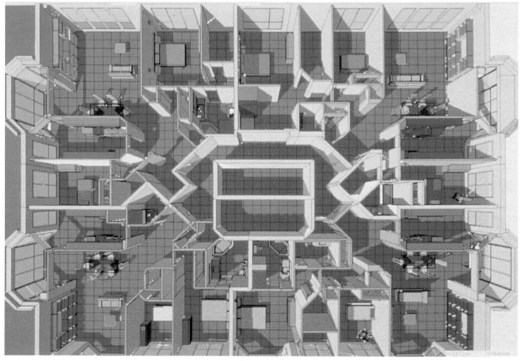

8 – 16 Rendered
perspective by Antoine
Fatio. Computer graphic
(Architrion II and Studio 8).
Beach House, Clement
Difillippo, Architect.

8 – 17 Rendered plan view
by Antoine Fatio. Computer
graphic (Architrion II and
Studio 8). WGMK office
renovation. Barretta and
Associates, Architects.

ARRANGEMENTS

Traditional drawings are arranged so that we see them in relationship to each other in a way that is not normally the case. Elevations of a building, arranged in a serial fashion encompassing the whole building, allow us to compare and contrast the different elevations and to see them as a set of interrelated, intricate parts. Elevations can also be arranged within a space or as a sequence of elevations at the edge of a space, or they may be laid down adjacent to different sides of a plan so that one sees the details of the plans and the elevations in close proximity to each other, gaining some notion of their direct relationship.

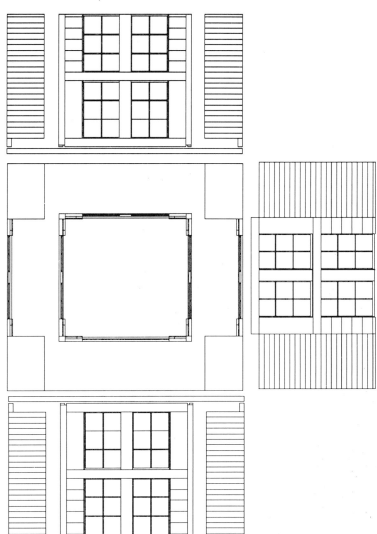

8 – 18 Composite drawing
of plan and elevations.
Computer graphic
(Architrion).

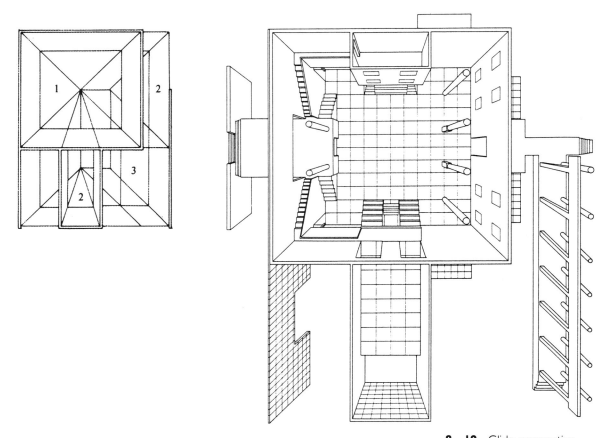

8 – 19 Glide perspective by Michael Garber. Ink. Core component glide view, from *Glide Perspective* by Kevin Forseth.

GLIDE PERSPECTIVE

On the basis of Renaissance models, Kevin Forseth has developed a comprehensive approach to bridging the gap between paraline projection and perspective drawings. The term *glide perspective* is derived from the abandonment of a single viewpoint for a perspective drawing in favor of multiple viewpoints along an axis, a glide path for the viewer. Parallel projection drawings assume the viewer might be at any number of positions at a fixed distance from the object. Perspective drawings place the viewer at one position in relationship to the object. Glide perspective provides a compromise between the paraline and perspective conventions by setting a fixed number of viewpoints in front of the object. While some glide perspectives have a complexity that would warrant the use of a computer-driven perspective generation program, it is possible to understand the basic principles and apply them freehand.

8 – 20 Glide perspective by Kevin Forseth. Ink. Freeform assembly of lateral armatures, from *Glide Perspective* by Kevin Forseth.

8 – 21 Glide perspective by Michael Garber. Ink. Double herringbone glide section, from *Glide Perspective* by Kevin Forseth.

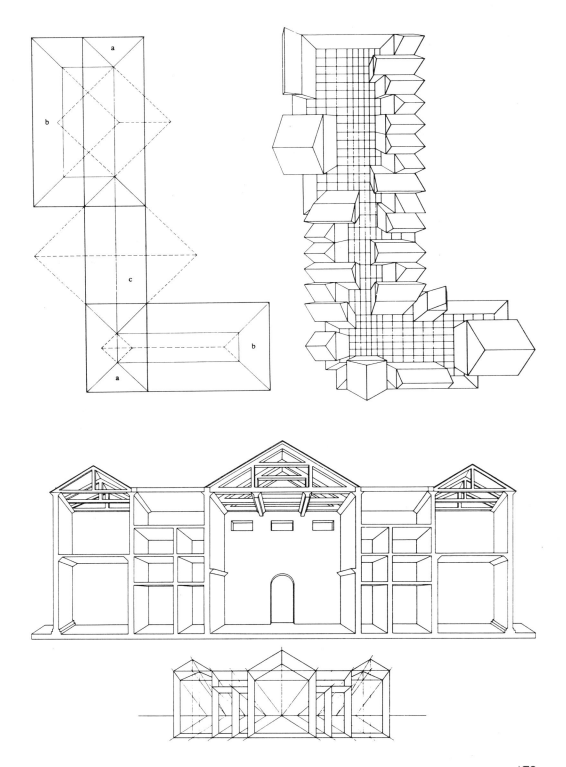

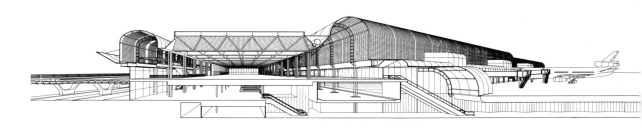

8 – 22 and 8 – 23 Split perspective projections by Murphy/Jahn Architects. Ink. United Airlines Terminal I Complex, O'Hare International Airport, Chicago, IL. Murphy/Jahn Architects.

SPLIT PROJECTION

While the basic perspective convention assumes a single directed view, the experience of environment is not always so simple, even from a single viewing position. In these cases designers can represent multiple view directions in a single drawing, conveying simultaneous experiences at a point in space and time. Like glide projection, split projection uses multiple vanishing points but is based on a single rather than multiple viewing positions.

CURVED AND PANORAMIC PROJECTIONS

While looking in a fixed direction, the cone of vision within which we can see objects clearly is about sixty degrees. While our peripheral view takes in a much wider scene, objects outside the sixty-degree cone remain fuzzy and indistinct. In normal experience, however, our view is not fixed; our eyes and heads are constantly shifting, providing a survey of the environment. Curved and panoramic projections are used to include those objects normally outside of our direct field of view, those things within our peripheral view, within a single drawing. The configurations used are similar to those produced by a wide-angle or fish-eye camera lens. Our view of objects in this wider-angle representation shifts from the perpendicular, as in elevation, to the parallel, as in perspective, and the result is a curved projection.

8 – 24 Illustration by W. Douglas Cooper. Pencil. Two Doors, from *Drawing and Perceiving* by Douglas Cooper with Raymond Mall.

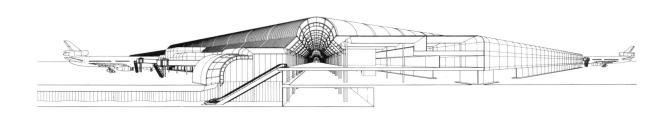

8 – 25 Reverse perspective, based on photo montage by David Hockney, by Paul Lew. Felt pen.

REVERSE PERSPECTIVE

This means of environmental representation, developed by David Hockney, is less an exact geometry for projecting space and more a collection of techniques intended to represent the experience of the viewer placed in the middle of space, rather than observing space from the outside as though looking through a window. In the basic perspective convention, space and objects diminish in size when they are at greater distances from us. We see the world as through a camera separating us from what we see. The parallel line projection brings us a step closer, increasing our sense of relationship to the environment by placing us and all objects in the environment at the same scale. Reverse perspective attempts to move us into the environment so that it encompasses us. Hockney tries to capture the experience of being surrounded by environment, as opposed to taking a picture of the environment. He fragments the normal view, then selectively alters the scale and position of the pieces so we can simultaneously experience environment as both distant and engulfing.

Cathi House uses a similar though less dramatic approach in her sketches, rendering selected objects in equal detail regardless of their distance from the viewer in conventional perspective. These drawings evoke the sensations we have when moving about environments and selectively focusing on near and distant objects.

8 – 26 Reverse perspective, based on drawing by Jim Stutzman. Computer graphic (Image Studio). MuseHouse. Stutzman & Associates, Architects.

8 – 27 Leisure sketch by Cathi House. Felt pen on newsprint. My Brother's House. House + House, Architects, San Francisco.

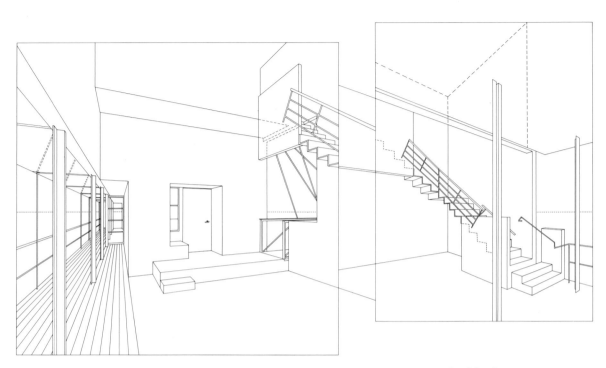

8 – 28 Sequence perspectives by Steven Holl. Ink. Cleveland House. Steven Holl, Architects.

MONTAGE AND OTHER COMBINATIONS

In the montage, conventional drawings are arranged in a loose pattern that attempts to convey more of the feeling of a space than its specific geometrical or physical description. A montage would not follow normal conventions of perspective or paraline projection.

Other combinations include a variety of conventions, such as plan/section perspective or orthographic or paraline projection. They allow us to free our view of a project from the constraints of any one specific convention and bring the different drawing approaches into close proximity, giving us an opportunity to shift perceptions and to take fresh views of the project.

8 – 29 Drawing by Yim Chan. Ink. A Temple for Lao-Tzu, from *Carleton Book*, Carleton University, School of Architecture, 1986.

8 – 30 Drawings by Lilly Chi. Ink. Suzhou Garden, from *Carleton Book*, Carleton University, School of Architecture, 1986.

185

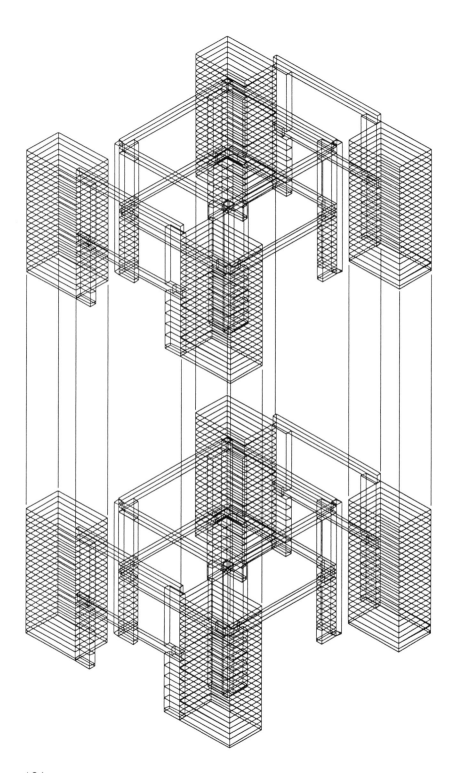

Wire-frame paraline
projection. Computer
graphic (Architrion).

CONCLUSION

We are in a time of great turmoil and change in the field of graphic representation, which presents us not only with problems but with a great number of opportunities and challenges. Throughout this book I have mentioned the new tools that computer and video technology provide that enhance visualization, and so, thinking and designing. The availability and ease of use of these tools is now shifting the discussion of drawing options from that of technique or craftsmanship to the realm of media and communication. In the future the consideration of drawing options will be focused less on the technology of drawing options and more on the relationship between media and human action and effectiveness. The concern for the so-called impersonality or coldness of the electronic media, particularly computers, may make us more aware of the emotional requirements of communication. Architects deal with an environment that not only affects people's lives intellectually but often has a profoundly emotional impact as well. If we are to address those emotional needs, we must understand the way in which those emotional aspects are translated or communicated through media. We also must understand the impact of emotional needs on our interactions with others and apply what we have learned in order to communicate more effectively.

BIBLIOGRAPHY

BOOKS ON DRAWING

Beittel, K. *Mind and Context in the Art of Drawing.*
New York City: Holt, Rinehart and Winston, Inc., 1972.

Bellis, Herbert F. *Architectural Drafting.*
New York: McGraw Hill, 1971.

Bonsteel, D. L. and Sasanoff, R. *An Investigation of a Televised Image in Simulation of Architectural Space.*
Seattle: University of Washington, 1977.

Bowman, William J. *Graphic Communication.*
New York: John Wiley & Sons Inc., 1968.

Burden, Ernest. *Architectural Delineation: A Photographic Approach to Presentation.*
New York: McGraw Hill, 1971.

Ching, Francis D. K. *Architectural Graphics.*
New York: Van Nostrand Reinhold Company, 1975.

———. *Architecture: Form, Space, & Order.*
New York: Van Nostrand Reinhold Company, 1979.

———. *Drawing: A Creative Process.*
New York: Van Nostrand Reinhold Company, 1990.

Cooper, Douglas with Raymond Mall. *Drawing and Perceiving.*
Silver Spring, MD: Information Dynamics, Inc., 1983.

Crosley, Mark Lauden. *The Architect's Guide to Computer-Aided Design.*
New York: John Wiley & Sons, 1988.

Czaja, Michael. *Freehand Drawing, Language of Design.*
Walnut Creek, CA: Gambol Press, 1975.

DeVries, Jan Vredeman. *Perspective.*
New York: Dover Publishing, 1968.

Downer, Richard. *Drawing Buildings.*
New York: Watson-Guptill Publications, 1962.

Doyle, Michael E. *Color Drawing.*
New York: Van Nostrand Reinhold Company, 1981.

Dubery, John and John Willats. *Perspective and Other Drawing Systems.*
New York: Van Nostrand Reinhold Company, 1972.

Edwards, Betty. *Drawing on the Right Side of the Brain*.
Los Angeles, CA: J. P. Tarcher, 1979.

Forseth, Kevin. *Glide Perspective*.
New York: Van Nostrand Reinhold Company, 1984.

Forseth, Kevin with David Vaughan. *Graphics for Architecture*.
New York: Van Nostrand Reinhold Company, 1979.

Franck, Frederick. *The Zen of Seeing*.
New York: Random House, 1973.

Garrett, L. *Visual Design: A Problem Solving Approach*.
New York City: Reinhold Publishing Company, 1967.

Goldstein, Nathan. *The Art of Responsive Drawing*.
Englewood Cliffs, NJ: Prentice-Hall, Inc., 1973.

Goodban, William T. and Jack Hayslett. *Architectural Drawing and Planning*.
New York: McGraw-Hill, 1972.

Guptill, Arthur Leighton. *Drawing with Pen and Ink*.
New York: Reinhold Publishing Company, 1961.

Hanks, Kurt and Larry Belliston. *Draw! A Visual Approach to Thinking*.
Los Altos, CA: William Kaufmann, Inc., 1977.

Hanks, Kurt, Larry Belliston and Dave Edwards. *Design Yourself*.
Los Altos, CA: William Kaufmann, Inc., 1977.

Hayes, Colin. *Grammer of Drawing for Artists & Designers*.
New York: Van Nostrand Reinhold Company, 1969.

Hill, Edward. *The Language of Drawing*.
New York: Prentice-Hall, Inc., 1966.

Hogarth, Paul. *Drawing Architecture: A Creative Approach*.
New York: Watson-Guptill Publications, 1973.

Jacoby, Helmut. *New Architectural Drawings*.
New York: Praeger Publishers, 1969.

————. *New Techniques of Architectural Rendering*.
New York: Praeger Publishers, 1971.

Kemper, Alfred M. *Drawings by American Architects*.
New York: John Wiley & Sons, 1973.

————. *Presentation Drawings by American Architects*.
New York: John Wiley & Sons, 1977.

Kliment, Stephen A. *Creative Communication for a Successful Design*.
New York: Watson-Guptill Publications, 1977.

Laseau, Paul. *Graphic Problem Solving for Architects and Designers*.
New York: Van Nostrand Reinhold Company, 1987.

————. *Graphic Thinking for Architects and Designers*.
New York: Van Nostrand Reinhold Company, 1980.

Lin, Mike W. *Architectural Rendering Techniques: A Color Reference*.
New York: Van Nostrand Reinhold Company, 1985.

Lockard, William Kirby. *Design Drawing*.
Tucson, AZ: Pepper Publishing, 1975.

————. *Design Drawing Experiences*.
Tucson, AZ: Pepper Publishing, 1975.

————. *Drawing as a Means to Architecture*.
New York: Reinhold Publishing Company, 1968.

Lockwood, Arthur. *Diagrams*.
New York: Watson-Guptill Publications, 1969.

McGinty, Tim. *Drawing Skills in Architecture*.
Kendall/Hunt Publishing Company, 1976.

McKim, R.H. *Experiences in Visual Thinking, 2nd Ed*.
Monterey, CA: Brooks/Cole Publishing Company, 1972.

Meier, Richard. *Richard Meier Architect*.
New York: Oxford University Press, 1976.

Mendelowitz, David M. *A Guide to Drawing*.
New York: Holt, Rinehart and Winston, 1976.

Murgio, Mathew. *Communication Graphics*.
New York: Van Nostrand Reinhold Company, 1969.

Nelms, Henning. *Thinking with a Pencil*.
Berkley, CA: Ten Speed Press, 1981.

Nicolaides, K. *The Natural Way to Draw*.
Boston, MA: Houghton-Mifflin, 1941.

O'Connell, William J. *Graphic Communications in Architecture*.
Champaign, IL: Stipes Publishing Company, 1972.

Oles, Paul Stevenson. *Architectural Illustration: The Value Delineation Process*.
New York: Van Nostrand Reinhold Company, 1979.

Oles, Paul Stevenson (Ed). *Architecture in Perspective III*.
Boston: American Society of Architectural Perspectivists, 1988.

————. *Drawing the Future: A Decade of Architecture in Perspective Drawings*.
New York: Van Nostrand Reinhold Company, 1988.

Porter, Tom. *How Architects Visualize*.
New York: Van Nostrand Reinhold Company, 1979.

Rottger, Ernst & Dieter Kiante. *Creative Drawing: Point & Line*.
New York: Van Nostrand Reinhold Company, 1963.

Stegman, George K. *Architectural Drafting*.
Chicago, IL: American Technical Society, 1966.

Thiel, Phillip. *Freehand Drawing, A Primer*.
Seattle, WA: University of Washington Press, 1965.

Walker, Theodore D. *Perception and Environmental Design*.
West Lafayette, IN: PDA Publishers, 1971.

————. *Plan Graphics*.
West Lafayette, IN: PDA Publishers, 1975.

Weidhass, Ernest R. *Architectural Drawing and Construction*.
Boston, MA: Allyn & Bacon, 1974.

Welling, Richard. *Drawing with Markers*.
New York: Watson-Guptill Publications, 1974.

————. *The Technique of Drawing Buildings*.
New York: Watson-Guptill Publications, 1971.

White, Edward T. *Concept Sourcebook*.
Tucson, AZ: Architectural Media, 1975.

————. *A Graphic Vocabulary for Architectural Presentation*
Tucson, AZ: Architectural Media, 1972.

————. *Presentation Strategies in Architecture*.
Tucson, AZ: Architectural Media, 1977.

VISUAL THEORY BOOKS

Arnheim, Rudolf. *Visual Thinking*.
Berkely, CA: University of California Press, 1971.

Bach, M. *Power of Perception*.
Garden City, NY: Doubleday, 1966.

Chomsky, Noam. *Language and Mind*.
New York: Harcourt-Brace, 1972.

Collier, G. *Form, Space, and Vision*.
Englewood Cliffs, NJ: Prentice-Hall, 1972.

DeBono, E. *Lateral Thinking*.
New York: Harper and Row Publishers, Inc., 1972.

Feldman, Edmund Burke. *Art as Image and Idea*.
Englewood Cliffs, NJ: Prentice-Hall, 1967.

Gibson, James. *The Perception of the Visual World*.
Boston, MA: Houghton Mifflin, 1950.

Harlan, C. *Vision and Invention*.
Englewood Cliffs, NJ: Prentice-Hall, 1970.

Huxley, A. *The Art of Seeing*.
Seattle, WA: Madrona Publishers, 1975.

Klee, Paul. *The Diaries of Paul Klee 1898-1918*.
Berkeley, CA: The University of California Press, 1964.

Koestler, Arthur. *The Act of Creation*.
New York: Macmillan, 1964.

McKim, Robert H. *Experiences in Visual Thinking*.
Monterey, CA: Brooks/Cole, 1972.

Parameter, Ross. *The Awakened Eye*.
Middletown, CT: Wesleyan University Press, 1968.

Samuels and Samuels. *Seeing with the Mind's Eye*.
New York: Random House, 1975.

DRAWING REFERENCE

Birkerts, Gunnar. *Gunnar Birkerts: Buildings, Projects and Thoughts*.
Ann Arbor, MI: The University of Michigan, College of Architecture, 1985.

Chang, Ching-Yu (Ed.). *Mitchell/Giurgola Architects Process Architecture. No. 2*.
Tokyo: Process Architecture Publishing Company, Ltd., 1977.

DaVinci, Leonardo. *Notebooks*.
New York: Dover Publishing, 1970.

Ehrman B. Mitchell and Romaldo Giurgola. *Mitchell/Giurgola Architects*.
New York: Rizzoli International Publications, Inc., 1983.

Eisenman, Peter. *House X*.
New York: Rizzoli International Publications, Inc., 1982.

———. *Peter Eisenman House of Cards*.
New York: Oxford University Press, 1987.

Hockney, David. *David Hockney: A Retrospective*.
Los Angeles, CA: Museum Associates, Los Angeles County Museum, 1988.

Moore, Charles and Kent Bloomer. *Body, Memory, and Architecture*.
New Haven, CT: Yale University Press, 1977.

Muramoto, Katsuhiko and Stephen Parcell. *Carleton Book*.
Ottawa, Canada: Carleton University, School of Architecture, 1986.

Pedretti, Carlo. *A Chronology of DaVinci's Architecture after 1500*.
Geneva: E. Droz, 1962.

Peña, William M., Caudill and John Focke. *Problem Seeking*.
Houston, TX: Candill Rowlett Scott, 1969.

Polshek, James Stewart. *James Stewart Polshek—Context and Responsibility*.
New York: Rizzoli International Publications, 1988.

Sellars, Beth and Glenn Davis. *Morphosis: A Decade of Architectural Confrontation*.
Spokane, WA: Cheney Cowles Museum, 1989.

Steinberg, Saul. *The Labyrinth*.
New York: Harper & Brothers, 1960.

Uy, Bon-Hui. *Architectural Drawings and Leisure Sketches*.
Honolulu: Bon-Hui Uy, 1978.

———. *Drawings: Architecture and Leisure*.
Mt. Kisco, NY: Bon-Hui Uy, 1980.

INDEX